You're All Invited

You're All Invited

Margot's Recipes for Entertaining

Margot Henderson

Photography by Joe Woodhouse

FIG TREE
an imprint of
PENGUIN BOOKS

FIG TREE

Published by the Penguin Group
Penguin Books Ltd, 80 Strand, London WC2R 0RL, England
Penguin Group (USA) Inc., 375 Hudson Street, New York, New York 10014, USA
Penguin Group (Canada), 90 Eglinton Avenue East, Suite 700, Toronto, Ontario, Canada M4P 2Y3
(a division of Pearson Penguin Canada Inc.)
Penguin Ireland, 25 St Stephen's Green, Dublin 2, Ireland (a division of Penguin Books Ltd)
Penguin Group (Australia), 250 Camberwell Road,
Camberwell, Victoria 3124, Australia (a division of Pearson Australia Group Pty Ltd)
Penguin Books India Pvt Ltd, 11 Community Centre,
Panchsheel Park, New Delhi – 110 017, India
Penguin Group (NZ), 67 Apollo Drive, Rosedale, Auckland 0632, New Zealand
(a division of Pearson New Zealand Ltd)
Penguin Books (South Africa) (Pty) Ltd, Block D, Rosebank Office Park,
181 Jan Smuts Avenue, Parktown North, Gauteng 2193, South Africa

Penguin Books Ltd, Registered Offices: 80 Strand, London WC2R 0RL, England

www.penguin.com

First published 2012
1

Copyright © Margot Henderson, 2012
Photography copyright © Joe Woodhouse
Arnold & Henderson photography © Martin Cohen and others at Arnold & Henderson

Designed by Nathan Burton

The moral right of the author has been asserted

All rights reserved
Without limiting the rights under copyright
reserved above, no part of this publication may be
reproduced, stored in or introduced into a retrieval system,
or transmitted, in any form or by any means (electronic, mechanical,
photocopying, recording or otherwise), without the prior
written permission of both the copyright owner and
the above publisher of this book

Set in Berling
Printed in China
Colour Reproduction by Altaimage

A CIP catalogue record for this book is available from the British Library

ISBN: 978–1–905–49060–8

www.greenpenguin.co.uk

MIX
Paper from
responsible sources
FSC
www.fsc.org   FSC™ C018179

Penguin Books is committed to a sustainable
future for our business, our readers and our planet.
This book is made from Forest Stewardship
Council™ certified paper.

ALWAYS LEARNING   **PEARSON**

For my darling dearest Fergus, thank you

Contents

Introduction 9

BREAD 15

BREAKFAST 25

LUNCH 41

   Soups 42
   Salads 56
   Snacks or quick bites 74
   A lunch feast with toast 82
   Comforting lunches 96
   Sunday and Christmas lunches 106

DINNER 131

   Feeding the masses 132
   Pasta, polenta and risotto 150

CELEBRATORY DINNERS 165

   Something to start with 166
   Main courses 174
   Vegetables 196

PUDDINGS AND CAKES 211

CHEESE 249

PARTIES 253

   Drinks 254
   Canapés 268

PICNICS AND BARBECUES 291

LIST OF MENUS 306

Index 310

Acknowledgements 319

Introduction

I have loved cooking for other people since I was a child growing up in the suburbs of Wellington, New Zealand. My mother was passionate about the new healthy way of living that had filtered across from America in the 60s with Dr Gayelord Hauser, which meant that when I was two everything white and refined was thrown out and the kitchen cupboards were filled with raw sugar, brown flour and kelp. The boiler cupboard always had yoghurt and yeast reacting away in it. Cider vinegar and honey was our cordial, and molasses was as giddy as it got. Mum was so passionate about our roughage levels that our packed lunches for school were brown bread 'crusties', sunflower seeds and raisins, which we would secretly swap for chocolate biscuits, but I was also very proud and loved our healthy food. My brothers struggled with it more. They were desperate for a loaf of sliced white bread.

That was when it all began: I think I was slightly greedy (chefs often are), but also my mother was such a health nut and I wanted to have biscuits, not bran. So the first recipe I attempted was the famous ginger crunch from the *Edmonds Cookery Book* (the New Zealand household bible). I was about ten, Mum and Dad were out, and I had decided to bake – not even knowing what cream, butter and sugar were – so I took the top of the milk out of the bottles in the fridge and ended up with a great messy sludge and nothing-at-all-looking ginger crunch. My first catering job was my little brothers' birthday party; Mum was hopeless, so I decided to step in and ordered white flour and sugar and started baking meringues, jellies, hokey pokey, toffee . . . and organizing games with prizes, of course. It was a great success, white sugar and all.

Then there were the snails. When I was studying French at primary school we had to collect snails from our gardens: we drowned them for several days and then the teacher cooked them up in the classroom with breadcrumbs and garlic. I never forgot it, the smell, the taste – they were delicious. I would be given snails in tins for my birthday and I was always cooking them for my mother's dinner parties – which was quite unusual for the suburbs of New Zealand.

Mum wrote a series of books on restaurants in Wellington and Christchurch, and she would often take us to glamorous restaurants where we would have serious French food – frogs' legs, flambéd oranges – quite old school, from the carpets to formal waiters with the dessert trolley, and cheese on trolleys too. I loved the food, and how the place and the surroundings were so much part of the whole experience. I started getting obsessed by restaurants.

During the 70s we ate a lot of lamb with salad, huge salads in big pottery bowls, brimming with every available ingredient: cabbage, leaves, raisins, nuts, cheese, vegetables, it was all in there, even fruit (though I have never been keen on fruit in my salads). Having dinner with a French family who lived up the road from us was a revelation. It was the first time I experienced the beauty of simple food, and the idea of less being more. A salad consisted of one type of leaf – looking back I feel it must have been something like butterhead lettuce – with a Dijon mustard dressing, which impressed me.

Once I started working in restaurant kitchens, I quickly found I enjoyed the restaurant life. In a way it is almost addictive. The family atmosphere – we are all in this together. No matter what, we are going to have to get through this together and hopefully in one piece, with happy customers. I have been inspired by many wonderful chefs, working alongside them, cooking their recipes, eating their food and of course reading their books. Cookbooks have been part of all my cooking.

I met Fergus Henderson while working at the Eagle in Farringdon. It seemed obvious that we should open a restaurant together. I had met him once before, in a pop-up eating club he had with Piers Thompson and Orlando Campbell; I ordered pigeon and peas and that is what I got – pigeon and peas. It seemed so simple and so perfect. I quickly fell for his food and for him. Within moments we had opened the French House Dining Room in Soho, along with Jon Spiteri. Maître d' extraordinaire. Cooking with Fergus was an eye-opener: instead of boning and stuffing, we were leaving things whole, garnishes were gone. It all made perfect sense.

Love and food all happened quickly. I met Melanie, Jon's wife, on their wedding day, just before we opened the French. My first English wedding – beautiful sunny day, long tables in the country and endless food. Babies followed, and when Fergus and Jon went off to open St John it seemed perfect that Mel and I run the French House Dining Room together.

The business was flexible enough, in a messy sort of way, to allow us to be mothers while working, and the children grew up in the French, running around the kitchen. The chefs were very patient. A few galleries started to ask us to do private dinners and we saw a way to extend the business. A lot of our catering style comes from the obvious – eating in restaurants, and of course our families and how they have fed large numbers. Fergus's parents, Brian and Elizabeth, are brilliant hosts. The welcome is warm, the table is beautiful, large tables squished with happy eaters, candles twinkling, the food delicious, and always the right dish, plenty of cheese and your glass is never empty. Most important.

Melanie and I ran the restaurant at the French House for seven years, but we lost it when the owners wanted to take it back and we found ourselves suddenly with no business and no income. For the next couple of years we cooked from the kitchen of my flat in Covent Garden – we cooked for 500 people from there, using the windowsills as fridges in the winter, which was hard – and I thought I was going to lose a husband.

Then an old friend, James Moores, bought the Rochelle School, a group of three Victorian buildings erected in the 1880s in East London, to use as spaces for young creative businesses, and was looking for somebody to run a canteen there, the hub around which the building revolved. While the renovations were happening, we catered out of various rooms in the school, dragging our equipment with us. We changed our catering name to Arnold & Henderson about this time; we liked the formality of it, sounding like a firm of solicitors. Now that we had space and professional kitchens our business took off – lots more lovely art world, weddings, dinners, travelling.

When Rochelle first opened we just had one communal table: it was a lovely scene, with the few people who knew about us sitting together, while the two of us ran around like mad things. We never really knew if anyone was going to ring the doorbell and come in, but they did. The Canteen doesn't have a licence and we're not allowed to open in the evening, so the catering is really important: the two businesses look after each other.

The most important thing I have learned about catering is that the result has to look effortless. It should feel generous, warm and relaxed. Fun also, of course, and stylish. That's what people like about Arnold & Henderson: there's a sense that it all seems so simple, as if they could almost have done it themselves – but they didn't have to.

Of course home entertaining is very different from restaurants and catering. It's a powerful position to be in, welcoming people to your home, and looking after them. It's a lovely thing to give to people: these big cities disperse us, and it's nice to bring everyone together. I love having people round and cooking at home. When you're catering for people it's a performance, but when I cook at home I don't have to perform, so it's a much more relaxed position to be in.

You have to put more hard work in when entertaining at home. You are doing everything, so you have to be organized: there's a lot of footwork, you have to do all the shopping and, most importantly, plan ahead. Think about how much space you have: I don't often make puddings at home – we have a little kitchen and it gets messy. We're a one-course-and-cheese family.

I like organized chaos when entertaining. You want everything to be in place so that you can sit down and have a few drinks and not end up doing too much. It's awful when your host is stuck in the kitchen slaving away and not having a good time. I prefer it, and I think people are more relaxed, if things aren't too formal: relaxed chaos.

There is a place for a round table but I prefer a long table, and not too wide. We don't just talk to the people sitting to our left and right these days, and if you're sitting at a round table you can't talk across it, you can only talk to the people on either side of you. It doesn't matter if you're a bit squashed. The most important thing about eating is being together and having a conversation. Obviously, good food can help that along but it's not everything.

I think placement is important at big dinners or weddings, because it makes everyone meet each other and makes you work harder than if you're sitting next to your nearest and dearest. You can always talk to them later. And it's much better for flirting.

Flowers and candles are best low – you want everything to be low so you can have lots of eye contact. Decorations work well if they flow, with a sort of scatter effect, a bit like planting bulbs in your garden – not too perfect, not too even. I love the sense that the flowers have just been picked from the garden (obviously they haven't, and someone has spent hours arranging them) – a classic fabulousness rather than twined grass and pebbles in the bottom of the vase.

Although I do love a glamorous meal with white table linen, a lovely floral tablecloth really makes me feel at home. I love all those French fabrics with tiny flowers on them but they don't really make them any more. For a wedding we catered recently we bought a roll of cloth from Ikea that was white with little blue flowers on it. It was for 300 people and we just rolled it up. You want the table to be light, and you want to be able to see the food. If your food looks dark and gloomy no one will want to eat it. You shouldn't be scared of your food. And you shouldn't be scared of the table.

Most importantly though, there shouldn't be any rules.

BREAD

We have been buying the bread for our restaurant from St John Bakery for years now. For large parties we order the long white loaves and pile them high, almost like a bread shop, in the dining room. A big pile of bread can soften a room.

They use the best flours; the white is unbleached and so has a little fleck of brown in it. It is a wonderful moment when a large delivery of bread arrives fresh from the bakery and the loaves are crackling away, or 'speaking' to you, as a baker would say.

But at home it's lovely to make your own bread for breakfast, lunch or dinner. I have always enjoyed making bread – it's such a soothing pastime. If you're unhappy, make a loaf of bread and it will make you smile. It's brilliant that something starting from such a humble beginning becomes something of such necessity; every table needs a good loaf of bread.

The following recipes are all very easy and quite quick. Dried yeast works well, so always have a few packets in the cupboard.

We always serve bread with meals. We cooked a big meal for Anselm Kiefer a few years ago in Paris. There were two long beautiful tables running down the middle of a metal factory. The guests were very glamorous, especially the women, slim and beautifully dressed. We wondered if they would eat, and they ate loads of everything, especially the bread; they were screaming for more bread.

Easy Bread

I love making bread. The pleasure is in the mess, the kneading, the watching, the smell, then that wonderful moment when your beautiful brown loaf comes out of the oven. When life is frantic and chaotic, as it often seems to be, and when things are crumbling about you, there is nothing more steadying than kneading dough.

The following recipe will give you a good, straightforward, no-fuss result. Kneading is a continuous motion. Grab one end of the dough, then pull it out and towards you. Stretch, fold and push. Keep repeating this movement – there should be a gentle loving rhythm to it.

MAKES 2 LOAVES

750ml warm water
20g fresh yeast or 2 level tablespoons dried yeast
1kg strong white bread flour
250g plain wholemeal flour
25g sea salt

Put 100ml of the warm water into a small bowl and add the yeast. Set aside to rest in a warm place for 10 minutes. The yeast will start to react and become frothy. Put the flours and salt into a large bowl and make a well in the middle. Pour in the yeast mixture and the remaining warm water and mix together. Once the dough has come together, it should be pliable and slightly sticky.

Turn the dough out on to a floured work surface and knead for 10 minutes. Place it in a lightly floured or olive-oiled bowl, cover with clingfilm and leave to rise in a warmish spot for about 1 hour, or until the dough has doubled in size.

Take the dough out of the bowl and knead again for 8 or so minutes. Divide it in half and shape it into 2 loaves. Place them on a floured or lightly oiled baking tray, cover with clingfilm, and leave to rise in a warm place until they have almost doubled in size again.

Preheat the oven to 180°C/fan 160°C/350°F/gas 4 and bake the loaves for 40 minutes. Tap the bottom of each loaf: they should sound hollow, and not make a dense thud. Leave to cool on a rack.

Brown Bread

1.3kg wholemeal bread flour
150g wheat germ
  (if you can't find wheat germ, you can substitute 50g oats)
550ml warm water
a few tablespoons of oil

For the yeast mixture
1 tablespoon dried yeast
2 tablespoons wholemeal bread flour
1 tablespoon molasses
500ml warm water

Stir the ingredients for the yeast mixture together in a bowl and cover with clingfilm. Leave for 20 minutes in a warm place. Once the mixture starts frothing it's ready.

Put the flour and wheat germ into a mixing bowl and stir in the yeast mixture with a wooden spoon. Slowly add the water and mix well. The consistency should be firmer than cake mixture, but too moist to knead.

Grease two 1kg loaf tins with a little oil and spoon the mixture into the tins until they are about three-quarters full. Cover with a damp tea towel or clingfilm and leave in a warm place to rise for 1 hour.

Preheat the oven to 200°C/fan 180°C/400°F/gas 6. Put the loaf tins into the oven and bake for 15 minutes, then reduce the heat to 180°C/fan 160°C/350°F/gas 4 and continue to bake for another 45 minutes.

The loaves should fall out of the tins quite easily; if not, scrape around the edge with a knife to loosen them. The bread should sound hollow when you tap the bottom. Leave to cool on a rack.

Soft Buns

If you want to bake these buns for breakfast, make the dough the evening before and leave it in the fridge overnight.

MAKES 24 SMALL BUNS

2 eggs, lightly beaten
1½ teaspoons instant fast-action dried yeast, or a 7g sachet
100g unsalted butter, melted
75ml whole milk, plus extra to glaze
75ml warm water
1 tablespoon clear honey or sugar
1 teaspoon sea salt
350g strong white fine bread flour, plus extra for kneading
50g plain flour

Put the eggs, yeast, melted butter, milk, water, honey and salt into a bowl and mix to a smooth paste. Stir in 75g of the bread flour and allow to rise for 20 minutes. Add the rest of the flour and knead for a few minutes – you may need a little more flour, but you want it to be a very soft dough. Place it in a bowl, cover with clingfilm and leave for 1½ hours in a warm place, or overnight in the fridge, until doubled in size.

Once the dough has risen, place it on a floured work surface and knead it lightly for a couple of minutes. (If the dough has been in the fridge, let it stand for an hour before using.) Divide it into 24 smallish pieces, shape them into buns and place on an oiled baking tray. Set aside for about 30 minutes, until doubled in size again.

Meanwhile, preheat the oven to 200°C/fan 180°C/400°F/gas 6. When the buns have risen, brush each one with a little milk and bake in the preheated oven for 10–12 minutes. Cool them on a wire rack.

Focaccia

20g fresh yeast or 2½ teaspoons dried yeast
1 tablespoon sugar
1.2 litres warm water
1.5kg strong white bread flour
125ml olive oil
150g mashed potato
2 teaspoons coarse sea salt

Put the yeast, sugar and 200ml of the warm water into a bowl and mix together. Leave in a warm place for 15 minutes. Once it is frothing a bit you know the yeast is working.

Put the flour into a large bowl and make a well in the middle. Pour in the yeast mixture and about two-thirds of the olive oil, then add the mashed potato and the remaining warm water and slowly bring it all together, using a spoon or your hand, until you have a wettish dough. Put the dough on a work surface and knead for 15 minutes – a little flour on your hands and the work surface will make this process easier.

Place the dough in a floured bowl and leave in a warm place for 45 minutes. It should double in size. Take it out of the bowl and knead it lightly for a couple of minutes, then lay it on a baking tray and leave it in a warm place to prove again for 45 minutes.

Preheat the oven to 180°C/fan 160°C/350°F/gas 4. Pinch the top of the dough all over, drizzle over the remaining olive oil and sprinkle with sea salt. Bake in the preheated oven for about 45 minutes, until brown and crisp on the top and bottom.

Corn Bread

I have been making this recipe for years, adapted from *Coyote Cafe* by Mark Miller. A book that teaches. I like to serve a piece of grilled corn bread with roasted or grilled tomatoes and a spoonful of green sauce. Or a grilled fish like mackerel, carefully picked off its frame, smeared over the toast with a little blob of crème fraîche and a squeeze of lemon. If you don't have any buttermilk to hand, use yoghurt instead.

MAKES 2 LARGE LOAVES

2 tablespoons olive oil, plus some
  for greasing the tray
2 red onions, peeled and sliced
1 fresh red chilli, thinly sliced
250ml warm water
1 x 7g packet of dried yeast
1kg strong white bread flour,
  plus extra for kneading

200g wholemeal plain flour
300g polenta or maize flour
  (masa harina)
1 tablespoon sea salt
250ml buttermilk
250ml whole milk
120g unsalted butter, melted
125ml cup corn oil

Heat the olive oil in a frying pan, then add the onions and chilli and cook for about 15 minutes, until very soft, almost mushy. Leave to cool slightly.

Put the warm water into a bowl and whisk in the yeast and 1 tablespoon of the strong flour. Leave in a warm place for 15 minutes, until it begins to froth.

Put the dry ingredients into a bowl. Make a well in the centre and stir in the wet ingredients. Add the onion mixture and the yeast mixture. Knead for 10 minutes on a well-floured surface, then put into an oiled bowl and leave in a warm place for 40 minutes, until doubled in size.

Shape the dough into 2 rounds. Lightly oil 2 baking trays and pop a loaf on to each one. Leave to relax for 15 minutes.

Preheat the oven to 180°C/fan 160°C/350°F/gas 4 and bake the loaves for 45 minutes, until when you pat the bottom they sound hard and hollow. Leave on a rack to cool.

Slice the bread while still warm if you can, and serve with lashings of butter or grilled with roast tomatoes.

Grape Bread

50g fresh yeast
450ml warm water
1kg plain flour
a pinch of sea salt
220g caster sugar
70ml olive oil
1.5kg grapes, the juicier the better
2 teaspoons verjuice or lemon juice
100g clear honey
2 sprigs of fresh rosemary

Crumble the yeast into a bowl and whisk in the warm water. Leave in a warm place for 15 minutes, until it begins to froth. Mix the flour, salt and 80g of the sugar together in a large bowl and make a well in the centre. Slowly pour in the yeast mixture and mix well. Turn on to a floured surface and knead for 10–15 minutes, until the dough feels elastic and bounces back when prodded. Oil a bowl with some of the olive oil and put in the dough. Cover with clingfilm and leave in a warm place for 30 minutes, until it has doubled in size.

Meanwhile, cut the grapes in half. Take the pips out (if not already seedless) and give them a rough squeeze. Put them into a bowl.

Once the dough has risen, preheat the oven to 180°C/fan 160°C/350°F/gas 4. Divide the dough in half and roll one piece out flat, about 1cm thick. Place it on a large oiled baking tray.

Add the rest of the sugar and the verjuice to the bowl of grapes and stir in 2 tablespoons of olive oil. Sprinkle half the grape mixture over the dough, then roll out the other piece of dough and place on top. Cover with the rest of the grape mixture and drizzle with the remaining olive oil. Bake in the preheated oven for 40–50 minutes.

While the grape bread is baking, put the honey into a small pan with the rosemary sprigs. Heat together for 5 minutes, then set aside. Take the grape bread out of the oven and leave to rest for 10 minutes. Cut into wedges and serve drizzled with the rosemary-scented honey.

Breakfast

- Eggs on Toast £4⁵
- Granola £3.⁵⁰
- Toast with Marmalad...
- Jam or Honey £2.
- Brownie £2.⁵⁰

Drinks

	IN	OUT
Tea	£ 1.50	1.50
Coffee	£1.80 - 2.70	1.50 - 1.8...

BREAKFAST

It's the first meal of the day, so if you are making breakfast for a crowd you need to think about the organization at least the day before – it's important to make sure you shop well, as that always makes a difference.

If it's a grown-up birthday breakfast, black velvets or Bloody Marys are essential. They help it all slip down, with a festive spring. The day before, make sure the champagne and Guinness are in the fridge or the Bloody Mary mix is made. Buy the happiest, loveliest free-range eggs and buy your avocados in advance, so that they have time to ripen. Poach fruits beforehand – they keep well in the fridge. Also, buckwheat pancake mixture can be made the day before and it actually gets better when it stands for a while; at the last minute you add the beaten egg whites. But if you do make the mixture the day before, you need to keep it in the fridge overnight otherwise it will over-rise and kill the yeast.

Set a beautiful table: cloths, napkins, cups and saucers, baskets of toast wrapped in napkins. Bowls of eggs, jars of preserves, jugs of hot frothy milk, pots of tea and good strong coffee, lots of choice to give the table glamour and excitement. It's one of the times of day when people's appetites vary – some can eat plates of bubble and squeak with eggs, while others may just want yoghurt and poached fruit. Personally I'm a toast and Marmite girl. Have you tried banana on Marmite and toast? It's a hot favourite with my family.

We serve breakfast at the Canteen: scrambled eggs, boiled eggs, poached eggs, Marmite and toast, yoghurt, granola. When we're doing breakfast for parties, with guests standing up, we usually just make smaller bits of everything so it's easy, and if it's a Sunday breakfast on a wedding weekend, we bring out the Solpadeine.

Marmalade

This recipe comes from a long line of cooks and chefs who all seem to have put their magic touch to it, beginning with Fergus's mum and finishing with my head chef, James.

MAKES 2.5KG

900g Seville oranges
5 lemons
2 litres water
2kg granulated sugar

Put the oranges and lemons into a very large pan and add the water. Bring to the boil, then reduce the heat a little and simmer for 2 hours. Remove the fruits from the liquid and set them aside to cool a little. Meanwhile, boil the liquid in the pan until reduced by a third.

Preheat the oven to 120°C/fan 110°C/250°F/gas ½. Put the sugar into a large heatproof glass bowl and warm in the oven for 15 minutes.

When the oranges and lemons are cool enough to handle, halve each fruit and spoon out the pulp and seeds, placing these in the middle of a large square of muslin. Tie the muslin with string to make a bag.

Slice the orange skins into thin strips and add to the liquid in the pan. Add the muslin bag, giving it a good squeeze to extract as much liquid as possible. Stir all the sugar into the liquid until dissolved.

Bring to the boil, then let the marmalade boil away for 10–15 minutes, until setting point is reached (105°C). If you don't have a thermometer, you can spoon a blob of marmalade on to an ice-cold plate; if you can make a valley with your finger, it has reached setting point.

Turn off the heat and leave the marmalade to settle for 5 minutes before ladling it into hot sterilized jars. Once opened, keep in the refrigerator.

Enjoy your marmalade with slices of toast. Steamed pudding and ice cream are some of my other favourite uses for marmalade.

Note: To sterilize jars, wash them well in hot soapy water, including the lids, then rinse in hot water and place on a baking tray. Place them in the oven at 180°C/fan 160°C/350°F/gas 4 for at least 10 minutes.

Eggs

Buy the best and freshest free-range eggs you can; this will give you the best results. They will give you better flavour, colour and texture and help with all your cooking skills.

Scrambled Eggs

3 eggs
a splash of milk or cream
sea salt and freshly ground black pepper
butter
toast

Put the eggs into a small bowl with a splash of cream and a sprinkling of salt and pepper, and whisk together. Heat a knob of butter in a pan and when slightly sizzling add the eggs. Cook on a low heat, stirring occasionally to bring them together. Have lots of hot buttered toast at the ready.

Poached Eggs

Fill a medium-sized pan with plenty of water. Add a pinch of salt and a teaspoon of white wine vinegar and place on the heat. When the water has an even gentle bubble, not too vigorous, use a wooden spoon or a whisk to stir the water in one direction, making a whirlpool. With the whirlpool very gentle, not at all vigorous, crack an egg into the centre. Sometimes it is helpful to crack it into a ramekin and then slide it into the swirling water. Cook for 3 minutes, until the yolk is firm. Remove with a slotted spoon, jiggling it to get rid of any excess water.

If you are cooking several eggs and want to use them later, you can keep them in cold water and then reheat them in hot water. Drain on kitchen paper. Pop them on to your sourdough toast, drizzle with olive oil, and sprinkle with a little freshly ground black pepper or a shake of togarashi (see page 32).

Spicy Fried Eggs

These eggs are from Kylie Kwong, the inspired chef from Sydney. They remind me of Leila Khattar's fried eggs in lamb fat. The fat she uses comes from lambs' tails. Both ways the eggs are fried in lots of oil or fat so you get bubbly, crisp whites.

1 spring onion
½ a fresh chilli
150ml olive oil
2 eggs
sea salt

Slice the spring onion and finely slice the chilli, scraping out the seeds. In a non-stick pan, heat the oil until it is slightly smoking. Crack the eggs in – mind you keep your face and hands well back, as the oil may spit quite violently. After a minute, turn down the heat and cook for another minute or so. You want a lovely crispy, bubbly white and a soft yolk. Serve on rice or toast. Sprinkle the eggs with the spring onions, chilli and sea salt.

Boiled Eggs

Boiled eggs are full of the joys of life. To avoid cracking, boil your eggs in a small pan – they don't need too much room, otherwise they roam about and smash into each other. Pricking them with a pin or a specially devised egg-pricker helps the pressure escape so they are less likely to crack. Also a gentle rolling boil or a strong simmer is what you need, as too much boiling will crack your eggs.

   Make sure you time your boiled eggs; this is not a moment for guessing. To avoid black-rimmed yolks in a cold egg, don't overcook them, and cool them quickly under running cold water.

Soft-boiled
Bring a pan of water to the boil. Prick the eggs, slide them into the simmering water, and turn the timer on for 4½ minutes. Serve straight away, with Marmite soldiers, lashings of coffee and freshly squeezed orange juice.

Hard-boiled
As above, but boil for 7–8 minutes, depending on how firm you like them. I like a little goo in my hard-boiled egg.

Bacon Buns

MAKES 24

24 slices of unsmoked streaky bacon, rind on
24 small buns
butter
ketchup, or fresh ripe tomatoes
brown sauce

Trim the rind off the bacon and gently fry in a pan until the fat has run.
Add your strips of bacon and fry until crispy.

Slice the buns, butter them, add the bacon and finish with ketchup
or brown sauce. I prefer a slice of raw tomato.

Avocado Toast

Prepare for this in advance and make sure that your avocados have had time
to ripen. Togarashi is a Japanese seasoning mix that you can buy in Waitrose.

SERVES 1 HUNGRY PERSON, OR 4 AS CANAPÉS

1 ripe avocado
½ a lemon
sea salt and freshly ground black pepper
2 slices of sourdough bread
ground paprika or togarashi

Halve and stone the avocado, slice into chunks, squeeze the lemon over and
season with salt and pepper. Squish on to the toasted bread and sprinkle with
paprika or togarashi.

Bubble and Squeak

A perfect breakfast dish for a weekend away with your pals and loved ones, when you're all cooking loads, eating loads and the fridge is brimming with leftovers. Preferably in a colder climate, though, maybe not on a hot summer holiday in Italy.

SERVES 6

2 tablespoons olive oil, plus some for frying the eggs
100g butter
2 onions, sliced into thin half-moons
1 leek, sliced into thin half-moons
100g pancetta or smoked streaky bacon, sliced
500g leftover mashed potato
250g leftover cooked greens, cabbage or Brussels sprouts, roughly chopped
6 cold cooked sausages, sliced
6 eggs

Preheat the oven to 180°C/fan 160°C/350°F/gas 4.

Heat the oil and half the butter in a heavy-bottomed ovenproof frying pan. When it's sizzling, add the onions and leeks and cook gently for about 20 minutes, until the onions have softened and browned.

Add the pancetta to the pan and cook for about 5 minutes, until it's browned and crisp. Add the leftover vegetables and the sausages. Keep cooking until a crust forms on the base, then turn everything over. Dot the remaining butter over the top and bake in the preheated oven for about 30 minutes, until brown and crisp.

When it's nearly ready, heat some olive oil in a non-stick frying pan and fry the eggs. Serve each person a spoonful of bubble and squeak with a fried egg on top and, of course, ketchup and brown sauce.

Buckwheat Pancakes, or Blinis

This fantastic recipe comes from *The Cake Bible* by Rose Levy Beranbaum. You can make the base the day before, and add the egg whites and cream just before making them. They are obviously best served with caviar. Now, in these sad times of fish shortages, we use a brand of farmed caviar. The farmers massage out the eggs and the fish swims on to make more.

These blinis can also be made larger, if you like, and can be served with a beetroot salad and crème fraîche. Keeps the veggies happy.

MAKES 20 MEDIUM OR 40 SMALL BLINIS

1½ teaspoons fresh yeast	½ teaspoon salt
½ teaspoon sugar	4 egg yolks
650ml warm whole milk	250ml double cream
125g buckwheat flour	2 egg whites
275g plain white flour	2 tablespoons butter

Start the day before, or at least 4 hours before you want to make the pancakes.

Put the yeast, sugar and 125ml of warm milk into a large bowl and whisk together. Cover the bowl with clingfilm and leave in a warmish spot until the mixture froths up – probably about 15 minutes.

Gradually stir in 375ml of the remaining warm milk and the buckwheat flour. It should be a smooth paste with a thick sauce-like consistency, not lumpy. Cover with clingfilm again, and leave in a warm place for 2 hours.

Stir in the white flour and salt, then add the remaining 150ml of warm milk. Whisk in the egg yolks, cover the bowl and leave for another hour or overnight in the fridge. The mixture will be thick with bubbles.

Whip the cream into soft peaks that stay up. Fold into the mixture. Beat the egg whites into soft peaks. Fold into the mixture.

Grease a large non-stick frying pan with a little butter. Drop tablespoons of the mixture into the pan and cook until little bubbles appear, then turn them and brown the other side. They take about a minute and a half each side.

Keep the pancakes warm in the oven while you make the rest.

Granola

This is my lovely mother's recipe. Mum has been making this since the beginning of my life. In the early 60s she discovered Dr Hauser and began a love affair with everything brown and healthy. All white ingredients went out of the window, and we ate only brown bread and molasses and kelp.

MAKES 12–14 PORTIONS

2 tablespoons olive oil
250g porridge oats
250g wheat germ
150g oatbran
4 tablespoons sunflower seeds
1 tablespoon golden linseeds

2 tablespoons pumpkin seeds
2 tablespoons sesame seeds
2 tablespoons desiccated coconut
65g chopped blanched almonds
2 tablespoons clear honey

Preheat the oven to 150°C/fan 140°C/300°F/gas 2.

Heat the oil in a large pan, then add all the dry ingredients and stir in the honey. Turn down the heat and cook for 10 minutes, stirring continuously with a wooden spoon. Spread out on a large baking tray and bake in the preheated oven for 10–15 minutes, stirring a couple of times. Serve with poached rhubarb and yoghurt or milk.

This also looks good as a canapé, in glasses or small paper espresso cups. Layer your mixtures with rhubarb and yoghurt and serve with a teaspoon.

Poached Dried Fruit

SERVES 8–10

500ml medium dry white wine
1 litre water
rind of 1 lemon, removed in strips
1 stick of cinnamon
4 cloves
125g organic dried apricots
125g dried pitted Agen prunes
125g dried pears
125g dried figs

Put the wine, water, lemon rind, cinnamon and cloves into a large pan and bring to the boil. Add the fruit, then turn down the heat, cover the pan and simmer for about 15 minutes, until the fruit is tender. Take off the heat and leave to cool.

When cool, pour into a jar or bowl and refrigerate. Serve cold, with yoghurt. This is also great as a pudding, warm, with crème fraîche, cream or custard.

Yoghurt

MAKES 1KG, TO SERVE 8–10

1 litre whole milk
200g good live plain yoghurt, alive with bacteria

Bring the milk slowly to the boil, then pour it into a large bowl and set aside until it has cooled down to 50°C (if you don't have a thermometer, this is hand-hot temperature). Stir in your yoghurt.

Cover the bowl loosely with clingfilm and put it in a warm place. My mother would always make our yoghurt in the airing cupboard, but if you don't have one, leave it in the oven overnight at 50°C.

When the yoghurt has thickened, keep it in the fridge. Serve with honey, poached fruit (see page 36) and granola (see page 35). Or use it for marinades and savoury dishes.

Poached (or Baked) Rhubarb

SERVES 6

1kg forced rhubarb, trimmed
200g caster sugar
200ml freshly squeezed orange juice
rind of 1 orange, removed in strips
1 cinnamon stick
2 star anise
1 vanilla pod, halved lengthways

Preheat the oven to 150°C/fan 140°C/300°F/gas 2, nice and low.

Cut the rhubarb into 4cm pieces. Put them into a baking tray and sprinkle them with the sugar. Pour over the orange juice and add the orange rind, cinnamon stick, star anise and vanilla. Cover with foil and bake in the preheated oven for 20–30 minutes, or until the rhubarb is tender.

Remove the orange rind, and scrape the seeds from the vanilla pod halves into the liquid. If there is a lot of liquid, and you want it thicker, you can remove the rhubarb with a slotted spoon, simmer the liquid to reduce it a little, then put the rhubarb back.

Mix with poached pears (see page 228) and serve with yoghurt for breakfast. Or with meringues and cream for pudding.

LUNCH

I'm a lunch person. My ideal lunch would always be something that somebody else cooks; though I do love to cook for others, something gentle and soothing. A pot of soup is always lovely. Smoked cod's roe with a cucumber salad makes a perfect summer lunch. It's a good meal to pick over. Saturday lunch often consists of Italian cold cuts and tomato salad followed by pasta or risotto, then pecorino and pears. Often we put lots of different dishes on to the table, a bit in the same way as a buffet, and they're very simple, and not plated, so you just take what you want from each thing (rillettes, pickles, terrine, salads, etc.). There is action, people are involved, they have to help each other, the table comes alive.

Any excuse will do for a big lunch, and even better if you have something to celebrate: a lunch that you know will end late with a beautifully messy table, a lunch that you know will not lead you back to work, that will take you on to more adventures. My birthday lunches have always been great treats, especially as May is such a lovely time of year in Britain. I love the gathering of friends, deciding what delicious treats we will have, how to dress the table, what to wear, more importantly what to drink. A special May lunch is normally piles of gull's eggs with celery salt, followed by platters of asparagus and hot butter, cheese and salad, and then, if it's a birthday, a cake. Washed down with bottles of chilled Fleurie.

Soups

Beetroot Soup

2kg small red beetroots, with stalks
2 onions
6 cloves of garlic
2 leeks
4 tablespoons olive oil
20g dried porcini mushrooms

1.5 litres vegetable or chicken stock
1 tablespoon red wine vinegar
sea salt and freshly ground black pepper
2 bunches of fresh dill
crème fraîche, to serve

Preheat the oven to 180°C/fan 160°C/350°F/gas 4.

Wash the beetroots. Remove the stalks and set aside. Put the beetroots into a roasting tray with 2cm of boiling water and cover with foil. Bake for approximately 1½ hours, until a knife slips in easily and the skin can be pushed off with your thumb. Let the beetroots cool down completely, then peel by rubbing the skin off. (It's best to wear surgical gloves for this job or you will have crimson hands afterwards.) Roughly chop the peeled beetroots and set aside.

Meanwhile, peel the onions, cut into thin slices, and peel and crush the garlic. Slice the leeks down the middle, discarding the outside leaves, and slice thinly. Slice the reserved beetroot stalks. Heat a good dollop of olive oil in a heavy-bottomed pan. Add the onions, garlic, leeks and beetroot stalks, then cover the pan and cook gently for about 40 minutes, the slower and longer the better.

While the vegetables are cooking, put the dried porcini into a bowl, pour over 300ml of boiling water, and leave them to soak for 30 minutes. Once they have softened, add them to the onion mixture, reserving the soaking liquid, and cook for 5 minutes. Add the chopped beetroot and the strained porcini soaking liquid, cook for about 10 minutes, then add the stock and vinegar. Simmer for a further 20 minutes. Take out the porcini, using tongs, and discard them, then whiz the soup in a food processor or blender and season with salt and pepper.

Pick the dill leaves and chop finely. Serve the soup in bowls, with a blob of crème fraîche and a sprinkling of dill, and with rye bread or Mum's brown bread (see page 18) on the side.

Aubergine and Red Pepper Soup

SERVES 8

4 large aubergines
6 tablespoons olive oil
sea salt and freshly ground black pepper
2 red onions, sliced
4 cloves of garlic, peeled and smashed
1 fresh red chilli, deseeded and sliced
4 vine-ripened tomatoes,
   roughly chopped

2 red peppers, deseeded and sliced
1 litre vegetable stock
1 lemon

To serve
300g natural yoghurt or labneh
   (Lebanese yoghurt)
chopped fresh mint (optional)

Preheat the oven to 190°C/fan 170°C/375°F/gas 5.

Halve the aubergines lengthways, then place them cut side up on a large roasting tray. Brush the cut sides with 2 tablespoons of olive oil and sprinkle with salt and pepper. Roast in the preheated oven for 20–30 minutes, until the aubergines have a good brown colour. Let them cool a little, then peel away the skin and roughly chop the aubergine flesh.

Heat the remaining 4 tablespoons of olive oil in a large pan, over a low heat, and add the onions, garlic and chilli. Cook gently until softened – about 15 minutes – then add the tomatoes and peppers. Cook slowly for a further 30 minutes, until the mixture becomes very unctuous and sloppy. Add the roughly chopped aubergine flesh and the stock and simmer for a further 30 minutes.

Leave the soup to cool a little, then either whiz in batches in a food processor or liquidizer, or use a stick blender in the pan. Add salt, pepper and a squeeze of lemon juice. Finish with a spoonful of yoghurt, or, if you can find it, labneh, and sprinkle with chopped fresh mint, if you like.

Celeriac Soup

A soup to soothe away any worry and gently fill your hungry winter stomach. It is a bowl of glamour, all pale and creamy. Truffle oil is always a cheeky addition at the end.

SERVES 6

4 tablespoons olive oil
2 onions, sliced
6 cloves of garlic, chopped
1 stick of celery, sliced
2 leeks, white only, sliced

2 heads of celeriac, weighing
  about 1.5kg altogether
1.25 litres ham stock
250ml single cream
sea salt and freshly ground black pepper

Heat the oil in a pan and add the onions, garlic, celery and leeks. Cook slowly – don't let them brown – for about 15 minutes, until tender.

Meanwhile, peel the celeriac and cut it into even hunks. Add it to the pan and cook very gently for a further 15 minutes. Once the vegetables have softened, add just enough stock to cover the vegetables and cook for a further 30 minutes or so, until all the vegetables are cooked. Stir occasionally.

Once cooled, whiz the soup in a food processor or liquidizer, or use a stick blender in the pan. Add more stock if necessary and stir in a little cream. Season well, and serve.

Minestrone

Perfect for a wintry lunch: minestrone is a meal on its own – all you need is loads of bread to sup it up with. It's also good housekeeping, as you can use up any bits that are lying around (it's always good to clear the fridge of all your old Parmesan rinds). You can replace the chard with cabbage, if you like.

SERVES 8–10

2 onions
6 cloves of garlic
1 bulb of fennel
50g dried porcini mushrooms
100ml olive oil
2 carrots
2 courgettes
a bunch of chard
3 pieces of leftover Parmesan rind

1 x 400g tin of tomatoes
2 large potatoes
2 litres chicken or vegetable stock
    (a stock cube is fine)
100g dried spaghetti, broken into pieces
100g green beans
sea salt and freshly ground black pepper
grated Parmesan, to serve

Peel and thinly slice the onions and garlic. Finely slice the fennel. Put the porcini into a bowl and pour on 250ml of boiling water, then leave to soak for 10 minutes.

Meanwhile, gently heat the oil in a very large pan. Add the onions, garlic and fennel and cook for about 20 minutes, until softened, stirring occasionally. Peel the carrots and courgettes, halve lengthways, then thinly slice and add them to the pan.

Wash the chard well and separate the leaves from the stalks. Slice the stalks thinly and add to the pan with the Parmesan rinds and tinned tomatoes. Cut the potatoes into 2.5cm chunks and add to the pan, then drain the porcini, reserving the soaking water, and add them too. Stir well, letting all the ingredients get to know each other. Cook for a couple of minutes.

Add the stock, then pour in the porcini soaking water through a fine sieve. Bring to the boil, then reduce the heat and simmer for 15 minutes.

Rip the chard leaves into manageable pieces and add them to the soup with the pasta and the green beans. Simmer for a further 15 minutes, until all the ingredients have come together and the pasta is cooked. Season with salt and pepper.

This soup is good left to get cold and reheated. Taste before serving and season again – don't forget to season. It keeps for several days in the fridge.

Serve in bowls, with a dollop of olive oil and some grated Parmesan.

Pumpkin Soup

Pumpkins have not been well thought of in Britain in the past, mainly because an inferior variety is grown that is only good for winter animal feed and Hallowe'en decorations. But the times are beginning to change, and pumpkins now come in all sorts of exciting varieties. My preferred variety is Crown Prince: it has olive green skin, and a rock-hard orange centre.

SERVES 8

1 green-skinned pumpkin, weighing about 1.5kg
2 tablespoons olive oil
2 onions, sliced
4 cloves of garlic, chopped
2 leeks, sliced
125ml white wine
1–1.5 litres vegetable stock
sea salt and freshly ground black pepper
1 x 300ml tub of crème fraîche, to serve (optional)

Cut the pumpkin in half or quarters, peel it and take out the seeds (you need a very sharp knife with some weight behind it, otherwise you are in for quite a struggle). Cut it into chunks, then into 3cm cubes.

Heat the olive oil in a decent-sized pan. Add the onions, garlic and leeks and cook gently for about 15 minutes, until the vegetables are soft. Pour in the wine, turn up the heat and let it bubble for about 2 minutes, until reduced a little. Add the pumpkin and cook for about 15 minutes, until it starts to soften. Add 1 litre of stock or water, enough to cover the vegetables, and simmer for 40 minutes on a low heat.

Transfer the soup to a blender a few ladles at a time and purée, adding a little more stock to thin it down if necessary. Season with salt and pepper and serve hot, with a dollop of crème fraîche if you like.

Leek and Potato Soup

Where would we be without a simple bowl of leek and potato soup? It will get you through any long afternoon. I think I am obsessed with potatoes in any shape or form. It's important to keep part of the dark green of the leek, otherwise you aren't really representing them properly, and try to buy young vegetables rather than old.

SERVES 8–10

6 leeks
2 onions
4 cloves of garlic
500g waxy potatoes
2 tablespoons olive oil
a bunch of fresh thyme
2 bay leaves
sea salt and freshly ground black pepper
2 litres chicken stock

Trim the leeks, then slice them down the middle. Cut them into half-moon chunks about 2cm thick, using both the green and the white parts. Peel and slice the onions. Roughly chop the garlic. Peel the potatoes and cut into happy hunks, about 2cm.

Heat the oil in a large pan and sauté the onions and garlic until softened, stirring now and again and keeping the heat low. Add the leeks, potatoes and the herbs, tied with string (this will prevent bits of herb messing up the pure leek and potato look).

Once the leeks have softened, which takes about 10 minutes, season with salt and pepper and add the stock, just enough to cover the vegetables. Simmer for 15–20 minutes, then remove and discard the herb bundle. Season again if necessary, and serve.

Tomato and Bread Soup

SERVES 6–8

250ml extra virgin olive oil, plus extra for serving
1 leek
1 bulb of fennel
8 cloves of garlic, thinly sliced
a pinch of dried red chilli flakes
1kg vine-ripened tomatoes, chopped
2 litres water or chicken stock
700g stale sourdough or other good bread, crusts removed
sea salt and freshly ground black pepper
10 fresh basil leaves
100g Parmesan cheese

Heat the olive oil in a large pan. Slice the leek and fennel thinly, add to the oil, and cook gently for about 5 minutes, until soft. Add the garlic and chilli flakes and cook for 2 minutes more, until softened, then add the tomatoes and cook for 10 minutes on a medium heat.

Add just enough stock to cover the tomatoes and simmer for 5 minutes. Cut the bread into small chunks, add to the tomatoes and simmer for a few minutes. Season with salt and pepper and stir in the ripped basil leaves.

Mix well, check again for seasoning, then serve with another drizzle of olive oil and freshly grated Parmesan.

Lemon Spinach Soup

This soup comes from Caroline Conran, via Elizabeth Henderson. It's a soup that fills you with energy and goodness.

SERVES 4–5

50g basmati rice (optional)
8 spring onions
500g spinach
850ml chicken stock
2 egg yolks
juice of ½ a lemon
sea salt and freshly ground black pepper
crème fraîche, to serve

Cook the rice, if using, then drain and set aside. Trim the ends off the spring onions and cut into small lengths, using both the green and white parts. Remove any tough stalks from the spinach.

Put the stock into a large pan, add the spring onions and simmer for 20 minutes, until tender. Add the spinach and let it wilt down for 5 minutes. Pour into a food processor or liquidizer and whiz until smooth (you may need to do this in batches), or use a stick blender in the pan.

Put the soup back into the pan over a low heat. Beat the egg yolks in a bowl and add 2 tablespoons of the soup; it shouldn't be too hot, otherwise the eggs will split. Add this egg/soup mixture to the soup in the pan, along with the lemon juice. Season with salt and pepper and continue to heat gently, but don't let it come to a simmer. Stir in the rice and serve with crusty bread and a dollop of crème fraîche. For a canapé party serve in little cups.

Fish Soup and Rouille

The fish stock takes time and trouble to make, but it's well worth it – you can use bought stock, but the results won't be as good.

SERVES 8

For the stock (makes about 1.7 litres)
1kg fish on the bone, for stock, e.g. red gurnard, carp, lemon sole (ask at your supermarket fish counter)
500g small crabs or crab claws
6 tablespoons olive oil
1 x 400g tin of chopped tomatoes
2 onions
2 bulbs of fennel
2 sticks of celery
2 leeks
1 whole bulb of garlic, halved horizontally
1 fresh red chilli
a bundle of fresh herbs, tied together, e.g. thyme, flat-leaf parsley
300ml dry white wine
1 lemon, halved

For the soup
4 shallots
2 bulbs of fennel
2 sticks of celery
2 leeks
4 cloves of garlic
2 tablespoons olive oil
2 teaspoons saffron
½ a 400g tin of tomatoes
75ml Pernod
1.7 litres fish stock (see left)

For the rouille
2 red peppers
6 cloves of garlic, peeled
juice of 1 lemon
50g ground almonds
20g fresh white breadcrumbs
½–1 teaspoon cayenne pepper
175ml olive oil
 sea salt and freshly ground black pepper

To serve
8 slices of easy bread (see page 16), toasted

To make the stock, first preheat the oven to 180°C/fan 160°C/350°F/gas 4. Gut the fish and clean all the fish heads, getting rid of the gills. Put the fish and crab into a large roasting tray and toss with 2 tablespoons of olive oil and the tinned tomatoes. Bake in the preheated oven for about 45 minutes – the bones should have some colour, but no burnt bits.

Roughly dice the vegetables. Heat 4 tablespoons of olive oil in a large pan and add the vegetables, garlic, chilli and herbs. Cook for about 30 minutes, until tender.

Smash up all the baked fish and crab from the baking tray and add to the pan of vegetables. Cook for a few moments, stirring as you go, then turn the heat up, add the wine and let it bubble for about 5 minutes, to reduce by half. Add the lemon halves. Add 2 litres of water, enough to cover everything, bring back to the boil, then reduce the heat and simmer uncovered for at least 1 hour. Remove any scum that appears on the top with a ladle.

While the stock is simmering, make the rouille. Preheat the oven again, to 200°C/fan 180°C/400°F/gas 6. Put the peppers on a baking tray and roast in the preheated oven for 50 minutes, then leave to cool. When cool, remove the skins and seeds. Put all the rouille ingredients apart from the olive oil, salt and pepper into a food processor and whiz together. With the motor running, slowly add the olive oil in a stream through the funnel as if you were making mayonnaise. Taste and add salt and pepper. Keeps well for a few days in a container in the fridge.

When the stock is ready, strain it in a colander, pushing as much of the fish through as you can (a potato masher works well here) – this is where all the flavour and body in your stock comes from. Set it aside until you need it.

To make the soup, slice the vegetables into thin half-moons, keeping them separate, and finely chop the garlic. Heat the olive oil, then add the shallots, garlic and saffron and sauté for 10 minutes, until tender. Add the rest of the vegetables and the tinned tomatoes and cook gently until soft and tender, for about 40 minutes. Add the Pernod and reduce rapidly for 1 minute, then add the fish stock and simmer uncovered for a further 40 minutes.

Serve the fish soup in big bowls, with a dollop of rouille and slices of toasted easy bread.

Salads

Cured Salmon with Cucumber, Mustard and Dill Salad

This salmon is also delicious with scrambled eggs. It's best to use organic farmed salmon if you can, but standard farmed salmon is fine too.

SERVES 6

150g coarse sea salt
150g caster sugar
125ml gin
a bunch of fresh dill, chopped
freshly ground black pepper
750g salmon fillet, skin on
  and pin-boned
lemon halves, to serve
buttered rye bread, to serve

For the cucumber, mustard and dill salad
1–2 cucumbers
sea salt and freshly ground black pepper
1 tablespoon Dijon mustard
1 tablespoon red wine vinegar
1 tablespoon caster sugar
juice of 1 lemon
100ml extra virgin olive oil
2 tablespoons chopped fresh dill

For this recipe you will need a large shallow plastic container. Put the salt, sugar, gin and dill into the container and grind in a good amount of pepper. Put the salmon into the curing mixture and turn it so that it is coated all over, leaving it skin side up. Cover tightly with clingfilm, or put a lid on the container, and refrigerate for 24 hours, turning the salmon several times.

Rinse off the curing mixture, then dry the salmon with kitchen paper.

To make the salad, peel the cucumber, then slice it in half and carefully deseed with a teaspoon. Cut into 0.5cm wedges, on an angle. Place the cucumber in a colander, sprinkle with a little salt, and set aside for 30 minutes.

Put the mustard, vinegar, sugar and lemon juice into a bowl and slowly add the olive oil, in a thin stream, whisking constantly. Stir in the dill and season with salt and pepper. Rinse the cucumber and add to the dressing.

Slice the salmon thinly and serve on a platter with the cucumber salad, lemon halves and buttered rye bread.

Butterhead, Lovage and Cucumber Salad

My business partner Melanie's favourite salad. The textures are gentle and soft, with no scratchy bits. Butterhead lettuce seems to have been put to one side by chefs for a few years, but it's making a comeback. Also lovage – God, I love it. My favourite herb, it looks fantastic in the garden and is easy to grow. (If you can't get hold of lovage, you can use flat-leaf parsley.) A happening salad bowl. Follow with cheese: Brie or Wigmore would be good.

SERVES 4

1 head of butterhead lettuce
a handful of fresh lovage leaves
1 cucumber, peeled or not, your choice

For the crème fraîche dressing
1 clove of garlic
2 teaspoons Dijon mustard

50g crème fraîche
1 teaspoon white wine
  or red wine vinegar
100ml olive oil
½ a lemon
sea salt and freshly ground black pepper

Go carefully now, you want the leaves as whole as possible. Wash and very gently pat dry the lettuce, watching out for slugs. Wash, dry and chop the lovage finely, with love. Using a mandoline, slice the cucumber thinly.

To make the dressing, chop or grate the garlic very finely. Put into a bowl with the mustard, crème fraîche and vinegar and whisk together, very slowly adding the olive oil a tiny bit at a time. Loosen with lemon juice if needed. Season with salt and pepper.

Once you have all the ingredients ready, mix the lettuce, lovage and cucumber together – put your hands deep into the bowl, lift and turn, but try to do this as little as possible. Too much fiddling with food wrecks it.

Dress with the crème fraîche dressing and serve.

Beetroot, Watercress and Red Onion Salad

Roast beetroot is wonderful mixed with chicory, watercress and a few ladles of lentils. Or topped with a spoonful of goat's cheese or curd, or a soft-boiled egg.

SERVES 6–8

1kg red beetroots
4 red onions
500g yellow beetroots
2 tablespoons olive oil
2 bunches of watercress

For the balsamic vinaigrette
6 tablespoons extra virgin olive oil
1 tablespoon balsamic vinegar
1 clove of garlic, finely chopped
1 teaspoon Dijon mustard
sea salt and freshly ground black pepper

Preheat the oven to 180°C/fan 160°C/350°F/gas 4.

Wash the red beetroots and trim the stalks, leaving a little stalky end. Place them in a baking tray, season with salt and pepper, and add about 5cm of boiling water. Cover the tin tightly with foil and bake the beetroots in the preheated oven for 50 minutes to an hour, or until you can easily slide a knife into the flesh.

Meanwhile, peel the red onions and cut them into wedges. Put them on a second roasting tray and add 2 tablespoons of olive oil. Season with salt and pepper and pop the tray into the oven alongside the beetroots for about 30 minutes, until the onions are soft.

When the beetroots are ready, take them out of the oven and let them cool down enough to handle. Then rub off the skins and cut the beetroots into wedges (best to put on some surgical gloves, otherwise your hands will be pink for days).

Whisk the vinaigrette ingredients together in a small bowl. Wash the watercress, pick off the leaves and spin them dry.

Peel the yellow beetroots and slice them thinly on a mandoline. Put them into a bowl and dress with a little of the vinaigrette.

In a large bowl toss together the red beetroot, yellow beetroot, roasted onions, watercress and dressing. Mix with your hands, then season with salt and pepper and serve.

Sprouting Broccoli and Anchovy Vinaigrette

As with many vegetables, the stalks of broccoli are as brilliant as their florets. Especially sprouting broccoli, though there is a moment when suddenly they are hard and stalky and not nice at all. They are great passed around at a party like asparagus – just be rigorous with the trimming.

SERVES 4–6

1kg sprouting broccoli, trimmed – get rid
  of anything that looks hard and old-bootish
anchovy vinaigrette (see page 73)

Once your veg is prepped and washed well, pop it into the fridge until you are ready to use it. Blanch for a few moments in a large pan of rolling, boiling salted water.

    Serve either tossed in the dressing, or in a dish with a bowl of dressing to dip into.

Braised Artichokes, Mint and Rocket

SERVES 4

16 violet globe artichokes
2 lemons
200ml olive oil
1 litre water
1 whole fresh red chilli
8 garlic cloves, peeled and left whole
a bunch of fresh mint
2 packets of rocket, washed and dried

For the dressing:
1 teaspoon Dijon mustard
1 teaspoon lemon juice
1 teaspoon sherry vinegar
a handful of fresh flat-leaf parsley
a handful of fresh mint leaves
a small handful of capers
50ml olive oil

To prepare the artichokes it's best to use a sharp paring knife and a good peeler. You also need a large bowl of water with a few lemons squeezed into it – this will keep the artichokes fresh and stop them discolouring while they are being prepared.

Clean the artichokes, cut off the top half, and snap away the outer leaves until you get to the light-coloured inner cone of leaves. Cut the prickly top end off. Trim the ends of the stems, but keep the stems long. Peel away the green at the base and along the stem. Keep the artichokes in the lemon water until you cook them.

Put the oil, water, chilli and garlic into a pan large enough for the artichokes to be placed upside down. Add the mint, stalks and all, and bring to the boil. Add the artichokes, then reduce the heat and simmer for 20 minutes, until tender. Leave to cool in the liquor.

Meanwhile, to make the dressing, whisk together the mustard, lemon juice and vinegar in a small bowl. Chop the parsley and mint and add to the bowl along with the capers. Finally, whisk in the olive oil.

When the artichokes have cooled down, slice them in half. Remove the tiny choke with a teaspoon and discard. Put the artichokes into a bowl and toss together with the rocket and the dressing.

The artichokes are also delicious served with roast tomatoes and broad beans when in season, or on their own. The possibilities are endless.

Smoked Mackerel, Potato and Watercress Salad

SERVES 4

4 smoked mackerel fillets
sea salt and freshly ground black pepper
250g new potatoes
2 bunches of watercress
a handful of fresh curly parsley, chopped finely
2 or 3 tablespoons vinaigrette (see page 73)

Check the mackerel fillets to make sure there are no bones left, then break them into large pieces. Leave to one side.

Bring a pan of salted water to the boil and cook the potatoes until tender. Drain, then leave to cool a little. When cooled, slice in half lengthways.

Trim the stalks off the watercress, wash and spin the leaves.

Put all the ingredients into a bowl and add the vinaigrette. Mix gently together – it's best to do this while the potatoes are still warm. Season with salt and pepper and serve with bread and butter.

Raw Asparagus, Fennel, Chicory and Pecorino Salad

We bought a box of large asparagus and decided that the best way to deal with them was raw in a salad.

SERVES 4

a bunch of fat asparagus, well trimmed
1 bulb of fennel
1 lemon
200g Pecorino cheese

2 heads of chicory
1 tablespoon capers
150ml lemon dressing (see page 72)
sea salt and freshly ground black pepper

Slice the asparagus and fennel very thinly and leave in icy, lemony water until needed. Shave the Pecorino. Slice the chicory and mix with the asparagus, fennel, cheese and capers.

Spoon over the lemon dressing, season with salt and pepper and serve.

Celeriac Rémoulade

A very sexy dish of creamy whiteness.

SERVES 6

250g crème fraîche
1 tablespoon Dijon mustard
1 tablespoon lemon juice

sea salt and freshly ground black pepper
1 celeriac, weighing about 650g
6 eggs, boiled for 6½ minutes

To make the dressing, mix the crème fraîche and Dijon mustard in a bowl, add the lemon juice, season with salt and pepper, taste, then maybe season a little more.

With a sharp knife, peel the celeriac. Using either a knife or a mandoline, cut into thin slices and then into very thin matchsticks. Mix with the dressing and serve a blob of the rémoulade on each plate, with a boiled egg alongside.

Fattoush with Chicken Wings

Fattoush is a salad from Lebanon; sumac has been a spice to discover. It comes from the berries of the sumac tree and has a refreshing lemon flavour. I first ate the most glorious Lebanese food when asked to breakfast with Leila Khattar. Leila is a brilliant cook and has often made wonderful breakfasts for us in her flat. The table would be covered with different dishes and more would appear. Fattoush was always refreshing and cleansing, almost helping you on with the next courses. Leila, come back to London and cook for us.

I hope in this recipe I haven't spoilt hundreds of years of culture. The chicken wings go well with this salad. Teenage food, lots of healthy salad to help with the spots and crisp wings to fill them up.

SERVES 6

For the chicken wings
500g chicken wings
6 cloves of garlic
juice of 2 lemons
70ml olive oil
1½ teaspoons sea salt
freshly ground black pepper

For the salad
12 radishes
1 bulb of fennel
4 tomatoes
4 spring onions
2 little gem lettuces

a bunch of fresh flat-leaf parsley
a bunch of fresh mint
a bunch of rocket
1 cucumber
2 sheets of flatbread
olive oil

For the dressing
2 cloves of garlic
4 teaspoons lemon juice
2 teaspoons ground sumac
70ml olive oil
1 teaspoon sea salt
freshly ground black pepper

Trim each chicken wing by chopping off the pointy end piece. Chop the garlic finely. Put the garlic and lemon juice into a bowl large enough to hold the wings, and whisk in the olive oil. Add the chicken wings and leave to marinate for at least 2 hours.

Preheat the oven to 180°C/fan 160°C/350°F/gas 4. Season the wings with salt and pepper, put them into a roasting tray, and roast in the oven for 40 minutes, until brown and crisp.

Meanwhile, to make the dressing, chop the garlic finely and put it into a bowl with the lemon juice, sumac and olive oil. Season with salt and pepper.

Slice the radishes thinly. Slice the fennel very thinly – a mandoline is helpful here. Dice the tomatoes into small chunks. Add all these to the dressing.

Thinly slice the spring onions and little gems and leave to one side. Pick the parsley and mint leaves and coarsely chop (they need to have texture), and roughly chop the rocket. Leave to one side. Slice the cucumber into quarters lengthways and then into small pieces.

When the chicken wings are nearly done, put the bread into the oven and toast until crisp. Break into small pieces and toss in olive oil.

When everything is ready, toss the salad together. Check for seasoning and lemon, and serve.

Dressings

Lemon and Crème Fraîche Dressing

This dressing is wonderful with butterhead, lovage and cucumber salad
(see page 59).

1 lemon
1 clove of garlic
1 teaspoon crème fraîche
1 teaspoon Dijon mustard
75ml extra virgin olive oil
sea salt and freshly ground black pepper

Squeeze the lemon juice and finely chop the garlic. Put the lemon juice, garlic,
crème fraîche and mustard into a cup or a small bowl and whisk together. Slowly
whisk in the olive oil, taste, and season with salt and pepper.

Lemon Dressing

2 lemons
100ml olive oil
sea salt and freshly ground black pepper

Squeeze the lemon juice, then put the ingredients into a bowl and whisk
together. Taste, and add more salt and pepper if necessary.

Vinaigrette

1 clove of garlic
1 teaspoon Dijon mustard
1 teaspoon verjuice
1 tablespoon red wine vinegar
100ml extra virgin olive oil
sea salt and freshly ground black pepper

Finely chop the garlic and put it into a small bowl. Whisk in the mustard, verjuice
and vinegar and finally whisk in the olive oil. Taste, and season with salt and pepper.

Anchovy Vinaigrette

1 small tin of anchovies
1 tablespoon capers
3 cloves of garlic
2 tablespoons red wine vinegar
140ml olive oil
2 shallots
sea salt and freshly ground black pepper
2 tablespoons chopped fresh flat-leaf parsley

Drain the anchovies, reserving the oil from the tin. Finely chop the anchovies,
capers and garlic and put into a bowl. With a small whisk or fork, stir in the
anchovy oil, vinegar and olive oil. Finely slice the shallots and add to the bowl.
Season with salt and pepper and stir in the parsley.

Snacks or quick bites

Rainbow Chard, Brown Rice and Tofu Tortilla

SERVES 4

500g chard
50ml olive oil
2 cloves of garlic, chopped
sea salt and freshly ground black pepper
200g cooked brown rice
100g silken tofu, cut into 2cm pieces
5 eggs

Preheat the oven to 180°C/fan 160°C/350°F/gas 4.

Pull the leaves away from each chard stalk. Wash the leaves and drain. Slice the stalks thinly. Separately blanch the stalks and leaves in boiling water, then refresh and squeeze out the water – especially from the leaves.

Heat a few tablespoons of oil in a pan, then add the chard stalks and cook for 4 minutes. Add the garlic, cook for a few moments, then add the chard leaves and season with salt and pepper. Mix in the rice and tofu.

Beat the eggs in a large bowl and stir in the chard mixture.

In a non-stick pan (with an ovenproof handle), heat 2 or 3 tablespoons of oil until smoking. Add the egg mixture and fry until the bottom is crisp. Slide a spatula underneath and flip the mixture over. Transfer to the oven to finish cooking for a further 10–15 minutes. Check if the tortilla's ready by pressing the top – it should be firm to touch.

Flip it on to a plate and serve for lunch.

Sweetcorn Fritters

Once the batter is made, use it straight away – don't be tempted to make it too far ahead of time, or the fritters won't be light and fluffy.

MAKES ABOUT 40 FRITTERS, TO SERVE 10

6 cobs of sweetcorn

200g medium cornmeal

200g plain flour

2 teaspoons baking powder

1 teaspoon sea salt

½ teaspoon freshly ground black pepper

1 teaspoon sugar

6 eggs, separated

750ml buttermilk

4 spring onions, finely chopped

2 tablespoons melted butter

100ml olive oil, for cooking the fritters

300g crème fraîche, for serving

Bring a very large pan of salted water to the boil. Add the sweetcorn, bring back to the boil, cover the pan and simmer for 8 minutes. Turn off the heat and leave the corn in the water for 10 minutes. Then drain and leave to cool.

Mix the dry ingredients together in a bowl and whisk the egg yolks and buttermilk in a jug. Make a well in the centre of the dry ingredients, pour in the buttermilk mixture, and whisk until combined. Slice the sweetcorn kernels off the cobs and stir them into the mixture with the spring onions and melted butter. Whisk the egg whites until they form soft peaks and fold them in. Check for seasoning and add salt and pepper if necessary.

Heat the oil in a large non-stick frying pan. When hot, plop several tablespoons of the corn mixture into the pan and cook for 5 minutes in total, turning halfway through, on a medium heat. The fritters should be golden brown on each side. Keep them warm in the oven while you make the rest, and serve with crème fraîche and a beetroot salad (see page 60).

Manea's Raw Fish

A dish from my childhood. Mum would often bring around friends who were from the Tokelau Islands, a small group of atolls in the Pacific Ocean. The women would arrive with lovely firm fresh fish, a coconut and a coconut grater. The grater would sit between their legs – with one crack the coconut would split in half and with beautiful curving movements they would shave out the coconut. It looked a lot easier than it was.

When I return home I always get Manea to make me her delicious raw fish. This is my version. Perfect on a hot summer's day.

SERVES 6

1 whole fresh coconut or 200ml tinned
  unsweetened coconut milk
2 green peppers
4 spring onions
2 tomatoes
1kg fresh white fish, filleted and skinned
  (a firm-fleshed fish works well for this,
  such as brill or halibut, and salmon
  fillet works well too; in New Zealand
  Manea uses warehou)

juice of 2 lemons
juice of 2 limes
50ml olive oil
sea salt and freshly ground black pepper
1 cos lettuce

Pierce the coconut and drain out the milk. Crack it in half and break the flesh away from the shell. Grate the coconut flesh on the large holes of a grater and leave to one side.

Slice the peppers thinly and the spring onions very thinly. Cut the tomatoes into thin slivers.

Make sure the fish is cleaned and has no bones or skin left. Cut it into 1cm thick pieces and put them into a bowl. Pour the lemon and lime juice over the fish and put into the fridge for an hour.

Put the coconut, peppers, onions and tomatoes into a bowl and add the olive oil, salt and pepper. Mix together, then add the fish and mix again. Taste for seasoning and put into the fridge for another 40 minutes.

Separate the leaves of the cos lettuce and serve the fish inside them.

Courgette Frittata

SERVES 8

6 tablespoons olive oil, plus a little for the pan
2 onions, chopped
4 cloves of garlic, finely chopped
8 medium courgettes
1 teaspoon sea salt
1 teaspoon ground paprika
12 eggs
freshly ground black pepper
20g soft butter

Heat the oil in a large frying pan, then add the onions and garlic and cook on a medium heat for 15–20 minutes, until very soft and sweet.

Meanwhile, preheat the oven to 180°C/fan 160°C/350°F/gas 4. Cut the courgettes into 1cm slices, and sprinkle them with the salt. Add them to the pan with the paprika and cook for a further 10 minutes, stirring frequently.

Beat the eggs in a large bowl and season lightly with salt and pepper. Add the courgette mixture. Heat the butter and a little oil in an ovenproof pan. Once the butter is frothing, add the egg and vegetable mixture. Cook for 5 minutes, until the base is sealed, then transfer to the preheated oven for 20–30 minutes, until the centre is firm, with a little give, and the frittata is browned on top.

Leave to cool a little, and cut into generous wedges to serve.

A lunch feast with toast

Duck Livers and Spinach on Toast

SERVES 2

250g duck livers or chicken livers
1 tablespoon unsalted butter
1 tablespoon olive oil
a splash of balsamic vinegar
a splash of chicken stock
1 teaspoon capers
a large handful of baby spinach
sea salt and freshly ground black pepper
1 clove of garlic
2 slices of sourdough toast

Ask your butcher for fresh plump livers – it's better not to get frozen ones. To clean the livers, cut away the gut bits and sinews using a sharp knife or scissors. Keep the livers whole.

Use a heavy pan with enough room for all the livers – you don't want them crammed in. They need to fry, not stew. Heat the butter and oil, add the livers and brown on each side over a medium high heat. Once they have a good colour, about 2–3 minutes on each side, add the balsamic vinegar and stock. Shuggle the pan, bringing the sauce together, then add the capers and spinach, season with salt and pepper, and toss.

Cut the garlic in half and rub the cut side over the toasted sourdough. Pour the livers and everything else in the pan over the toast and serve immediately.

Smoked Cod's Roe

What a fantastically simple dish, and beautiful too. With a butterhead and cucumber salad it makes a perfect summer lunch. Don't forget lots of icy white wine.

SERVES 6–12

sourdough bread (day-old bread will help the slicing)
olive oil
sea salt
500g smoked cod's roe
2 lemons
unsalted butter

Preheat the oven to 180°C/fan 160°C/350°F/gas 4.

Thinly slice the bread and place it on a baking tray. Drizzle with olive oil and sprinkle with sea salt. Bake in the preheated oven for about 4 minutes.

Now put it all on the table: the cod's roe and a sharp knife on a board, halved lemons in a bowl. Put the toast into a bowl wrapped in a napkin. Don't forget the butter. Now let everyone get stuck in, slicing what they want and making their own cod's roe toasts.

Smoked Cod's Roe
with Crème Fraîche

SERVES 8–10

500g smoked cod's roe, at room temperature
1–2 lemons
2–3 tablespoons crème fraîche
2 tablespoons extra virgin olive oil
sea salt and freshly ground black pepper
sourdough bread or baguette slices, to serve

Cut the cod's roe in half and scoop out the middle with a spoon. Place in a food processor, squeeze in the juice of 1 lemon, then turn on the machine and while whizzing add the crème fraîche and olive oil. Whiz for just a moment more, season with pepper, and add a little salt or more lemon juice if needed.

Serve on sourdough toast or long French bread slices, grilled with olive oil or baked in the oven (see page 86).

Rabbit Terrine

Start making this terrine two days before you need it.

SERVES 8–10

180g boned pork belly
2 tablespoons olive oil
4 shallots, finely diced
2 tablespoons fresh thyme leaves
4 cloves of garlic, finely chopped
125ml dry white wine
1 tablespoon cognac
400g boned rabbit meat, plus the
  rabbit liver if you can get it
200g chicken livers, trimmed

100g lardo or fatty pancetta
sea salt and freshly ground black pepper
zest of 1 lemon
200g pancetta, thinly sliced
  (about 24 slices)

To serve
gherkins or cornichons
toast

First of all, mince the pork belly finely. Put it into a large bowl and set aside.

Heat a little olive oil in a frying pan and gently cook the shallots, thyme and garlic for about 15 minutes. Once they have softened, add the wine and let it bubble and reduce. Lastly add the cognac and again, bubble and reduce.

Cut the rabbit meat, livers and lardo into 1cm pieces and add to the minced pork belly. Add the shallot mixture, salt, pepper and lemon zest and mix well. Test the seasoning by frying and tasting a little of the mixture.

Line the base and sides of a terrine dish, measuring about 30 x 10cm, with the pancetta slices, slightly overlapping, leaving enough hanging over the edge so you can fold it over the top later. Fill the terrine with the meat mixture, then fold the pancetta over so that the meat is completely covered and the whole thing looks neat and snug. Cover the terrine with foil and leave overnight in the fridge.

Preheat the oven to 150°C/fan 140°C/300°F/gas 2. Place the terrine inside a roasting tray and pour hot water into the tray to come halfway up the sides of the terrine. Cook for about 1 hour and 45 minutes. If you have a meat thermometer, the temperature in the centre when you test it should be 75°C.

Uncover and leave to cool, then put fresh foil on top, weight it down (a couple of tins of tomatoes works well), and refrigerate overnight.

Serve slices of the terrine with toast and cornichons. Or serve small cubes of the terrine on rounds of toast as a canapé, topped with a sliver of cornichon.

Rabbit Rillettes

Rillettes can be used as a canapé, a cold starter, or as part of a spread – we often serve a combination of small bowls of rillettes, toast, cornichons and salad when guests first sit down. It all makes for a happy exchange at the table.

SERVES 20–30 AS A CANAPÉ, 6–8 AS A STARTER

2 rabbits, weighing about 1.5kg each
2 tablespoons sea salt
½ tablespoon black pepper
a bundle of fresh thyme and bay leaves
2 bulbs of garlic, cloves peeled and lightly crushed
rind of 1 lemon, removed in strips
1kg pork belly
2kg duck fat

First, joint each rabbit into 8 pieces, or ask your butcher to do this. Put them into a bowl and season generously with the salt and pepper. Add the herbs, garlic and lemon rind. Chop the pork belly into even hunks. Pack the rabbit and pork belly snugly into a container and pop into the fridge for up to 12 hours, or overnight. Curing adds to the flavour, although you should watch out for curing the rabbit too long and making everything too salty.

Preheat the oven to 160°C/fan 150°C/325°F/gas 3. Brush off all the seasoning ingredients from the meat and place it in a large, deep roasting tin. Cover with the duck fat, then put the tray into the preheated oven and gently, gently poach your meat, submerged in glorious fat. Generally this takes about 4 hours.

Once the meat is collapsing off the bone it's ready to be picked. Take it out of the fat and leave it on a tray until cool enough to handle, then shred both meats together, discarding the bones. Season with salt and pepper and cover with the strained duck fat.

Rillettes are best served at room temperature. Store in the fridge, though, and remove a few hours before serving.

Kipper Pâté

When buying kippers look out for those with a lighter colour, as they will have a more gentle smoke flavour.

SERVES 6–8

2 kippers, smoked, weighing approx. 400–450g
175g cold unsalted butter
1 lemon
a few drops of Tabasco
sea salt and freshly ground black pepper

To serve
sourdough bread, toasted
lemon wedges

Preheat the oven to 180°C/fan 160°C/350°F/gas 4.

Put the kippers into a roasting tray, bone side up, and dot with about 50g of the butter. Bake in the preheated oven for 15 minutes. They should be moist and easy to pull apart. Leave to cool slightly.

Discard all the skin and bones, putting the kipper flesh into a bowl. Boning these little blighters is time-consuming, but if you carefully pull the frame away from the flesh, most of the bones will come away too. There are larger bones and finer ones. Best to go through the flesh several times. A good job to share – you can sip white wine and chat as you all carefully pick through the flesh.

Squeeze the lemon juice over the picked fish, tasting as you go, and add the Tabasco and the rest of the butter, chopped. With a fork, mash the butter and kipper flesh together – any fine bones that remain can be mushed in. Season with salt, if you need it, and pepper, and continue to fork the mixture together until you have a good consistency.

Store in the fridge, and bring to room temperature before serving on slices of sourdough toast with lemon wedges alongside.

Artichoke Heart and Berkswell on Toast

SERVES 4

sea salt and freshly ground black pepper
2 large firm green globe artichokes
1 clove of garlic
juice of 1 lemon
1 tablespoon truffle oil
1 tablespoon olive oil
150g Berkswell cheese
sourdough bread, toasted, to serve

Bring a large pan of water to the boil. Add a generous amount of salt, then put in the whole artichokes and cover with a lid slightly smaller than the pan, pushing it down so as to keep the artichokes from bobbing out of the water. Boil for about 30 minutes, until the leaves can be removed with a little tug and the centre can be pierced with a knife.

When cool enough to handle, remove all the leaves so you are just left with the hearts. Put all the ingredients except the cheese and bread into a food processor and purée for a few moments. Go carefully with the oil, as you don't want the mixture to be too wet. Season with salt and pepper. You may need to add a little more lemon.

With a peeler make lovely ribbons of Berkswell. Spread the artichoke purée on slices of toast, season with salt and pepper and finish with the Berkswell. Can be a canapé or a starter or snack.

Brandade

There is nothing better than a blob of white brandade. White food is very chic.

SERVES 6–8

250g salt cod fillets
a few sprigs of fresh thyme
2 bay leaves
2 lemons
200g potatoes

sea salt and freshly ground black pepper
150ml olive oil
2 cloves of garlic, bruised
100–150ml milk

Soak the salt cod in water for 24 hours, changing the water as many times as you can, or leave the cold tap running over the cod, to wash away as much salt as possible.

Put the fish into a pan, cover with fresh cold water, and add the thyme, bay leaves and half a lemon. Bring to the boil, then lower the heat and poach gently for 15 minutes, until the flesh flakes when touched. Remove the fish from the water using a slotted spoon and leave to cool. When cool enough to handle, remove the bones and skin and discard them. Set the fish aside.

Meanwhile, peel the potatoes and cut them into chunks. Bring a pan of salted water to the boil and cook the potatoes for 20–25 minutes, until soft and easily mashable. Drain, mash and leave to one side.

Put the olive oil into a pan with the whole cloves of garlic and heat for 5 minutes on a very low heat. Remove the garlic, which will have infused the oil. Squeeze the juice from the remaining lemon halves. Heat the milk until warm.

Whiz the fish in a food processor, slowly adding most of the warm olive oil and about 4 tablespoons of lemon juice through the funnel with the motor running. Once you have a smooth paste, remove it to a bowl and fold in the mashed potato, a little more oil and half the warm milk. Season with salt and pepper, and check to see if you need more lemon juice or warm milk to thin the consistency. It should be like a thick spreadable paste.

Brandade is best served warm but is great cold as well. For canapés, heat in a pan with a little more oil or milk and serve on toasted sourdough. For a main meal, reheat in the oven in Le Creuset type dishes until lightly browned on top. Serve with piles of toast in a basket wrapped in a tea towel or napkin, with a bowl of soft-boiled eggs. Radishes will also add a good crunch.

Comforting lunches

Fish Pie

This dish has been passed on to me from Elizabeth, my mother-in-law, via her son Fergus. He taught me to stop trying to jazz it up with prawns, salmon and leeks. Leave it. Enjoy its simplicity, its whiteness, its creaminess and its restorative qualities. It's important to make sure the eggs have a runny yolk.

Fish pie is about love and togetherness: a perfect dish for a gathering of friends and family. Its only problem is that it does use rather a lot of dishes and pans.

SERVES 6

400g undyed naturally
  smoked haddock fillet
400g fresh haddock fillet
1 litre milk
2 fresh bay leaves
6 peppercorns
½ an onion, roughly chopped
2 sticks of celery, cut in half
6 eggs

For the mashed potatoes
2kg potatoes (Desiree work well)
130g butter
100ml milk
sea salt and freshly ground black pepper

For the white sauce
100g butter
80g plain flour
reserved 1 litre of milk that the fish was
  cooked in (top up to 1 litre, if it's less)
sea salt and freshly ground black pepper

Preheat the oven to 180°C/fan 160°C/350°F/gas 4. Put the smoked and fresh haddock fillets into a baking dish and cover with the milk. Add the bay leaves, peppercorns, onion and celery. Cover with foil and bake for about 25 minutes, until the fish starts to give when prodded. Take out of the oven and leave to one side to cool. Leave the oven on if you are going to cook the pie straight away.

When cool enough to handle, lift the fish out and carefully, carefully remove and discard the bones and skin. Flake the fish into large pieces, trying not to break it up too much. Strain the milk into a medium pan, discarding the flavourings, and set aside.

Meanwhile, peel the potatoes, cut them into even-sized pieces and cook them in boiling salted water for 20–25 minutes. Heat the butter and milk in a separate small pan. Drain the potatoes and leave them in the colander for a few minutes to steam dry, then put them back into the pan, add the milk and butter, mash, taste and season with salt and pepper.

Boil the eggs in a pan that will hold them comfortably, but not with too much room, otherwise they will bang away at each other: bring a pan of water to the boil and carefully put the eggs in (you could prick them first with a pin so they don't crack when they hit the boiling water). Boil for 7 minutes, then run cold water over them to cool them down and prevent any discolouring. Shell the eggs and leave to one side.

To make the white sauce, melt the butter in a heavy-bottomed pan and stir in the flour. Keep stirring for about 3 minutes – there should be a biscuity smell. Heat the milk from cooking the fish that you have set aside, and gradually add to the butter and flour mixture a little at a time, constantly stirring with a wooden spoon. Bring to simmering point, then turn down to a very low heat and cook for a further 15 minutes, stirring frequently. Taste and season with salt and black pepper. This should give you a lovely creamy sauce.

Preheat the oven to 180°C/fan 160°C/350°F/gas 4 if it is not already on. To assemble the pie, arrange the fish over the base of a large baking dish. Cut the boiled eggs in half and scatter over the fish. Pour the white sauce over, leaving enough room to add a healthy layer of mash. With a fork fluff up the potatoes – this will make it pretty and crispy. Bake for 30–40 minutes, until well browned on top.

Remove from the oven and leave for a few moments to settle. Serve with frozen peas.

Salt Cod and Potato Bake

Salt cod and potato bake played an important part in the early days of my romance with Fergus, as it was the first dish that I cooked for him.

There are many ways to make this dish, but the recipe below is a Portuguese version I learnt from David Eyre at the Eagle. The most important thing about this dish is that it all comes together and has a lovely sticky texture.

SERVES 4

500g salt cod
a bundle of fresh herbs,
e.g. thyme, parsley
3 bay leaves
½ a lemon
1kg waxy potatoes (Desiree are good)

2 onions
4 cloves of garlic
125ml olive oil
sea salt and freshly ground black pepper
8 tomatoes, sliced
4 eggs, boiled for 8 minutes

Soak the cod for 24 hours, changing the water every few hours. Once soaked, pour away the water, then put the cod into a large pan and cover with fresh cold water. Add the bundle of herbs, the bay leaves and the lemon half. Bring to the boil, then reduce the heat and simmer for 15 minutes. Strain and leave to cool. Once cool, remove the bones and skin from the fish and put the flesh to one side.

Preheat the oven to 180°C/fan 160°C/350°F/gas 4.

Peel the potatoes, leaving them whole, and put them aside in a pan of water. Peel and slice the onions and garlic. Heat the olive oil in a heavy-bottomed pan, add the onions and garlic, then turn the heat down and cook gently until soft.

Slice the potatoes about 2mm thick on a mandoline or using the slicing attachment on a food processor, being careful of your fingers. Put them into a bowl, mix in the onion and olive oil mixture and season with salt and pepper.

Spread a third of the potato mixture in the bottom of a large baking dish. Cover with half the salt cod and add another third of the potato mixture. Layer the rest of the salt cod on top, followed by the sliced tomatoes. Finish with the remaining potatoes.

Bake in the preheated oven for approximately an hour, until the potatoes are cooked through – if they are browning too much, cover the dish with foil and turn the heat down. Serve each portion with a boiled egg.

Chorizo and Potato Stew, or Caldo Verde

This soup is hearty enough to be served on its own, the potato soaking up all the delicious flavours.

SERVES 4–6

100ml extra virgin olive oil,
   plus extra to serve
2 onions, sliced
4 cloves of garlic, chopped
6 cooking chorizo sausages
2 bay leaves

1kg waxy potatoes or new potatoes
750ml–1 litre chicken stock
sea salt and freshly ground black pepper
300g spring or winter greens,
   such as cavolo nero

Heat the olive oil in a large heavy-bottomed pan and cook the onions and garlic for about 15 minutes, until soft. Cut the chorizo into 2cm slices and add to the pan with the bay leaves. Cook everything together for about 15 minutes, until the sausages have a good colour and begin to release their oils. This is important, as the flavour comes from this first stage.

Peel the potatoes and cut them into slightly bigger pieces than the chorizo – it's better to have them a bit bigger so they don't collapse when they're cooked. Add them to the pan with just enough chicken stock to cover them, and simmer until they are cooked through. Season with salt and pepper.

Remove any very thick stalks from the greens, then roll the leaves into a bundle and slice thinly, using a very sharp knife. Just before serving, add the greens to the pan and simmer briefly until they wilt into the stew.

Serve in soup bowls, drizzled with olive oil.

Courgette, Mint and Butter Bean Stew

Lovely served with grilled or soft polenta.

SERVES 6–8

300g dried butter beans,
  soaked overnight
½ a bulb of garlic (from a
  bulb halved horizontally)
2 bay leaves
3 strips of lemon rind
8 medium courgettes
8 shallots

125ml extra virgin olive oil
6 cloves of garlic, sliced thinly
a pinch of saffron
1 tablespoon chopped fresh thyme
150ml dry white wine
sea salt and freshly ground black pepper
a handful of chopped fresh mint

Drain the soaked butter beans, then put them into a pan with plenty of fresh unsalted water and bring to the boil. Drain, then cover with fresh water and bring up to the boil again. Reduce the heat to a simmer and add the garlic, the bay leaves and 1 strip of lemon rind. Cook for 40–50 minutes, then remove from the heat and leave to cool in the liquid. When cool, drain the butter beans, reserving the cooking water. Set both aside.

Meanwhile, slice the courgettes at a jaunty angle, about 2cm thick. Peel the shallots and cut in half lengthways. Heat the olive oil in a large pan, then add the shallots and garlic and cook on a medium heat for about 10 minutes, until softened. Turn the heat up, add the courgettes, and cook for about 5 minutes, until they start to turn golden. Add the saffron, 2 more strips of lemon rind and the thyme.

Put a lid on the pan and cook for 10 minutes on a low to medium heat, then add the butter beans and the wine. Turn up the heat for a minute or two to let the alcohol evaporate, then lower the heat again and cook for 5 minutes, until the courgettes are soft. If you need more liquid, add a little of the reserved butter bean stock. Season with salt and pepper.

Sprinkle with the chopped mint, and serve.

Sunday and
Christmas lunches

Roast Forerib of Beef

Beef, glorious beef . . . and a favourite is White Park, the oldest breed. I managed to buy a hindquarter recently, one of the most loved animals I have ever encountered. They graze on the grass in a beautiful valley, coming inside only for the coldest months.

They are huge beasts, and it was quite an undertaking just to unload it from the van. Have a chat with your butcher about the cut of beef you are purchasing, as it won't be cheap. I prefer grass-fed than grain-fed. There should be a good marbling in the meat and the fat should be firm; check diets, breeds and ageing of the meat. It should be at least two weeks. It's best to have the joint chined, as this will make carving much easier. If it's not chined, roast it on the bone and carve the whole piece away from the bone before slicing.

SERVES 10–12

3kg beef forerib, on the bone
  and chined
2–3 tablespoons olive oil
sea salt and freshly ground black pepper

For the gravy
1 teaspoon Dijon mustard
200ml red wine
600ml chicken or beef stock

For the horseradish
1 fresh horseradish root
250g crème fraîche
juice of 1 lemon
sea salt and freshly ground black pepper

Take the forerib out of the fridge at least an hour before you want to cook it. You want the meat to be at room temperature when you start, especially if you like it rare.

Preheat the oven to 220°C/fan 200°C/425°F/gas 7. Rub your beef all over with a little oil, salt and pepper and put it into a roasting tray. Put it into the preheated oven and roast for 20 minutes, then turn the temperature down to 180°C/fan 160°C/350°F/gas 4 and cook for a further 2 hours and 10 minutes. Check by sliding a long thin knife into the centre of the meat, and if it feels warm when you hold the knife against your lip, it is ready. Wrap the meat in foil and leave it to rest for at least half an hour or even longer; an hour is good.

The meat will relax and retain the juices.

Once you have your beef safely resting to the side, take the roasting pan and place it over a medium heat on the stove. Add the mustard, wine and a little stock and whisk, loosening any yummy bits left behind in the tray. Add the rest of the stock and simmer to let it reduce down. Bubble away for a bit, then pour into a pan. Simmer for 20 minutes, then season and keep warm. If you haven't got stock tucked away, a chicken stock cube is brilliant.

While the gravy is simmering, peel and grate the horseradish, either by hand or in a food processor. Put it into a bowl and mix with the lemon juice, then stir in the crème fraîche. Season with salt and pepper.

Carve the meat, and serve on platters with the gravy in a jug, the horseradish in a bowl and piles of roast root vegetables (see pages 109–11).

Roast Roots

The following vegetables are all lovely roasted. We often have platters of roasted roots as finger food. Large platters of messy beautiful vegetables can be very impressive and delicious. When slicing them, always try to stay true to the form of the vegetable.

Preheat the oven to 180°C/fan 160°C/350°F/gas 4.

Celeriac

1 celeriac
6 cloves of garlic
olive oil
fresh thyme sprigs
sea salt and freshly ground black pepper

Peel the celeriac and cut it into 2cm thick hunks. Leave the garlic in its skin. Put into a roasting tray and mix with olive oil, enough to get a sizzle going. Scatter some thyme over, and season well with salt and pepper. Check the celeriac frequently and keep turning the pieces – you want them to be browned and evenly cooked.

Carrots

Young carrots straight from the garden, with slightly odd shapes, are best. Coat them in olive oil, salt and pepper, put them into a roasting tray and cook until tender.

Fennel

Take the tough outer leaves away, and slice the fennel bulbs into wedges lengthways. Coat them with olive oil, salt and pepper and put them into a roasting tray. Move them around while they are roasting so they don't stick to the pan. When they start to brown, add a little wine and cover with foil for a further 20 minutes.

Garlic

Roasting garlic can be done several ways: whole bulbs, or the cloves separated, unpeeled or peeled. It can be roasted along with the vegetables or just on its own. Anchovy dressing is very good with roasted garlic squished in.

Pumpkin

I use the light green acorn pumpkins – they roast very well, the flavour is sweet, the colour is a lovely orange and their texture is superior. The large orange-coloured pumpkins are dull, floury and tasteless. Best used for Hallowe'en.

With a large sharp knife, slice the pumpkin in half, scoop the seeds out, then slice into triangular wedges, leaving the skin on. Season with salt and pepper and put them into a roasting tray skin side down and roast until tender. If the pieces are reasonably small they can easily be picked up as finger food.

Butternut Squash

Much the same as for pumpkin. Slice in half, scoop the seeds out, decide on your preferred shape, season with salt and pepper, and roast until tender. Garlic and shallots can be roasted alongside the pumpkin and squash, making them all the more delicious.

Jerusalem Artichokes

Give them a good scrub, but leave the skin on. Cut them in half and roast them flesh side down in a roasting tray, sprinkled with salt and pepper. Turn them over halfway through – they are ready when they are brown and crisp on the outside and soft on the inside.

Parsnips

Peel, slice in half or quarters lengthways, then blanch in boiling water for 5 minutes. Mix about 75ml of olive oil with a little Dijon mustard and rub this over the blanched parsnips. Heat some oil in a roasting tray and add the parsnips – they need plenty of room. Bake until brown and crisp.

Roast Sirloin

Serve this with Dijon mustard, horseradish, celeriac mash and watercress. For a large party, serve it in little buns, with green sauce (see page 302).

SERVES 6

½ a sirloin of beef, trimmed
sea salt and freshly ground black pepper
vegetable oil

Take the meat out of the fridge at least half an hour before you want to cook it, so that the meat can come to room temperature.

Preheat the oven to 180°C/fan 160°C/350°F/gas 4. Generously season the sirloin with salt and pepper, especially the fatty side. Heat a heavy-bottomed pan until it is quite hot and add a little oil. Place the meat fat side down in the pan, then turn the heat down to a moderate temperature and brown the meat on all sides, pouring away the fat as it renders.

Once the meat is sealed all over, put it into a roasting tray and cook in the preheated oven for 15 minutes. Then turn the oven down to 140°C/fan 130°C/275°F/gas 1 and cook for a further 40 minutes. Check by sliding a long thin knife into the centre of the meat, and if it feels warm when you hold the knife against your lip, it is ready.

Leave the meat to rest for half an hour before serving. Or set aside to serve cold later.

Roast Pheasant

To avoid dry and stringy pheasant, I suggest you confit the legs separately.
Roast the breasts on the carcass and serve with braised sprouts (see page 117)
and baked stuffing scones (see page 125). Rather than just one brace, a pile of
breasts and legs will add to the air of festive celebration. If you have too much,
use the leftovers in a salad, or a pie, or even cheeky toasted sandwiches.

SERVES 16

4 brace of pheasant (8 pheasants)
sea salt and freshly ground black pepper
½ a bulb of garlic
a bundle of fresh herbs, e.g. thyme, sage, bay leaves
1kg goose fat
100g butter
1 tablespoon olive oil
2 ladles of chicken stock
75ml white wine

When buying your pheasants, try to choose ones that are dry to the touch,
rather than sticky. If they are packaged in dreadful plastic, whip them out and
wrap them in greaseproof paper – they will be happier with a little air getting
to them.

To joint the pheasants, first cut the legs off. Simply follow the hipbone and
cut through the joint. For the breasts, cut away the central part of the frame
(the spine) with either a sharp knife or kitchen scissors – both work well. The
breasts will still be attached to the frame, which will stop them shrivelling up
and help with flavour.

To confit the pheasant legs, preheat the oven to 90°C/fan 80°C/195°F/gas
¼. Find a heavy ovenproof dish that the legs will fit into snugly. Season the legs
with salt and pepper and place them in the dish with the half bulb of garlic and
the bundle of herbs. Melt the goose fat in a pan and pour over the pheasant
legs. Cook in the preheated oven for 1 hour, then leave to cool in the fat and
refrigerate until needed.

To roast the breasts, preheat the oven to 200°C/fan 180°C/400°F/gas 6. Heat the butter and oil in an ovenproof pan. Season the breasts with salt and pepper, place them breast side down in the sizzling pan and brown gently. Tip off the fat, then add a ladle of chicken stock. Transfer to the preheated oven with the confit legs and cook for 10–15 minutes.

Take the pheasant legs and breasts out of the pan and rest them on a plate. Put the pan with the juices over a medium heat and add another ladle of stock and the white wine. Simmer to reduce down to a sauce.

Carefully slice the whole breasts away from the frame and serve the breasts and legs on a platter, with the sauce poured over.

Braised Brussels Sprouts with Chestnuts

We used this recipe a lot back at the French House, serving the nutty greens with game or guinea fowl. There is quite a long prep time involved in cutting up the Brussels. As for the chestnuts, don't roast and peel them yourself, but buy them vacuum-packed and pre-peeled from a butcher's or a good food shop.

SERVES 4–6

1kg Brussels sprouts
150g pancetta
2 medium carrots
6 shallots
2 tablespoons goose fat
3 cloves of garlic
200g chestnuts, roasted and peeled or vac-packed
1 or 2 splashes of white wine
100ml chicken stock
sea salt and freshly ground black pepper

Trim the ends and outer leaves of each Brussels sprout, then roughly cut into quarters. Wash and leave to drain.

Cut the pancetta into small pieces. Slice the carrots in half down the middle and then into half-moon pieces. Cut the shallots into quarters lengthways.

Heat the goose fat in a pan. Add the pancetta and shallots and cook over a medium heat, stirring occasionally. After 5 minutes, add the carrots and garlic. Once they have softened and come together, add the Brussels sprouts, chestnuts and white wine. Simmer until the wine has reduced a little, then add the chicken stock. Season with salt and pepper and serve.

Roast Quails

Quails are a brilliant crowd-pleaser: they're straightforward to cook, they have a robust nature, which makes them difficult to overcook, and everyone loves them, especially kids. A large pile of quails with legs a-go-go make for a festive moment at any time of the year.

SERVES 6

2–3 tablespoons vegetable oil
12 quails
sea salt and freshly ground black pepper
50ml chicken stock

Preheat the oven to 200°C/fan 180°C/400°F/gas 6. Heat a little oil in a pan and carefully brown the breasts of each bird. Once they have a good colour, transfer them to a roasting tray, season them with salt and pepper, and add the chicken stock. Cook in the preheated oven for about 20 minutes, until lovely and brown.

Serve with lentils, roast pumpkin and watercress (see page 122).

Lentils, Roast Pumpkin and Watercress

Where would we be without lentils? Though I am sure a few vegetarian friends are bored with them. My cooking of pulses has changed so much since my vegetarian cooking days, when I would make piles of stodgy pulses. The cheffy undercooked variety is just as bad. I love a Puy lentil and all that sail with her: they should hold their shape but be soft and giving. They cook as well in stock as in water, and are a great vehicle for soaking all around them.

SERVES 4

2 onions
5 cloves of garlic, plus a whole bulb
70ml olive oil, plus some to serve
1 leek
250g Puy lentils
100ml white wine
1 litre chicken stock or water
½ a lemon
sea salt and freshly ground black pepper
½ an Acorn or Crown Prince pumpkin (roughly 800g)
a knob of butter
1 teaspoon Dijon mustard
a bunch of watercress

Peel and slice the onions and the 5 cloves of garlic, then put them into a deep sauté pan with half the olive oil on a moderate heat. Slice the leek into slim half-moons and add to the onions. Cook for about 15 minutes, until the vegetables are cooked through.

   Add the lentils, then pour in the wine and simmer to reduce a little. Cover with stock, or water if you want to go veggie. Add the lemon half and simmer gently for 40 minutes, until softened. Season with salt and pepper. Leave to cool.

Meanwhile, preheat the oven to 180°C/fan 160°C/350°F/gas 4. Cut the half pumpkin in half again and take out the seeds, then slice into thickish wedges. Leave the skin on, as it will hold together better that way. Rub with the remaining olive oil and arrange on a baking tray with the bulb of garlic, halved horizontally. Bake in the preheated oven for about 40 minutes, until soft (check by piercing with a knife).

Just before serving, reheat the lentils, adding a spoonful of olive oil, a knob of butter and the Dijon mustard. Wash and pick the watercress, so you have more leaves than stalks. Stir the pumpkin and watercress into the lentils, squeezing the garlic out of its skin.

A perfect autumnal dish, either with quails or on its own.

Roast Turkey

SERVES 10–12

1 x 6kg turkey, hopefully free-range
375g softened unsalted butter
zest and juice of 2 lemons
sea salt and freshly ground black pepper
400g streaky bacon, sliced
1 kg stuffing (see page 125)
a little water or chicken stock

For the gravy
about 600ml chicken or turkey stock
1 tablespoon plain flour
100ml white wine
sea salt and freshly ground black pepper

You can prepare the turkey several hours before it goes into the oven. Take it out of the fridge at least an hour before cooking, to bring it to room temperature.

Preheat your oven to 180°C/fan 160°C/350°F/gas 4.

Untruss the bird's legs. Put the softened butter, lemon zest, juice, salt and pepper into a bowl and squish together. Gently slide your hands in between the skin and flesh of the bird, separating the two. Make a thick blanket of the butter between the flesh and skin – this will help protect the breasts and legs and keep them moist. Season the skin with salt and pepper and cover with the bacon, like an overcoat.

Generously fill the inside of the bird with stuffing and place it in a roasting tray. Pour in some water or a little stock, to keep the juices flowing. Keep topping up the juices at the bottom of the pan so they don't burn, and baste away, once every hour or so. A 6kg bird with 1kg of stuffing should take about 4½ hours to cook, based on 40 minutes per kilo.

Check the bird is ready by piercing deeply into its thigh with a thin skewer – the juices should run clear. A meat thermometer, if you have one, should read 80°C internal temperature when you stick it in the thigh.

Move the bird on to a platter – don't be nervous, just lift and move. Wrap it in foil and leave it to have a decent rest, at least half an hour.

Tip the juices from your roasting tray into a jug and leave them to settle. Once the fat has risen to the top, skim it off and discard. You want to be left with only the lovely juices.

Meanwhile, heat the roasting tray over a medium heat, add a little stock and loosen any bits that are baked on to the bottom. Whisk in a tablespoon of flour. Then pour in the juices, turn the heat up a little, add a few splashes of white wine, and cook for a few minutes. Add a pint of stock and simmer, whisking until you have a smooth gravy. Season with salt and pepper and serve with the turkey.

Stuffing

1 tablespoon unsalted butter
1 tablespoon goose fat
4 medium onions, thinly sliced
2 cloves of garlic, finely chopped
1 leek, sliced into thin half-moons
2 tablespoons fresh thyme leaves, finely chopped
6 leaves of fresh sage, finely chopped
75ml port
200g vacuum-packed chestnuts
200g apples, peeled
1kg sausage meat
2 eggs
sea salt and freshly ground black pepper
500g sourdough breadcrumbs

Heat the butter and goose fat in a medium-sized pan. Add the onions and garlic and cook gently until softened, then add the leeks and chopped herbs and cook for a few minutes longer. Add the port and bubble away for a few moments. Cook until all is happy and unctuous.

Blanch the vacuum-packed chestnuts for a moment, still in their plastic, then take them out and chop them up roughly, along with the apples. The chestnuts need to be the same sort of size as the apples, to give your stuffing texture.

Put all the ingredients into a large bowl, adding the breadcrumbs last, and mixing as you go. The stuffing should be sticky and moist, not too dry.

If you have too much stuffing you can make stuffing scones. Just shape the mixture into smallish blobs and bake them on a greased baking tray for 20 minutes at 220°C/fan 200°C/425°F/gas 7 until firmish, brown and crisp. Keep warm until needed, or flash in the oven just before serving.

Roast Chicken

Simon Hopkinson's book *Roast Chicken and Other Stories* is a gem that everyone should own. If you have a copy, you can read his recipe, but if not, read on for my version, which is probably almost the same as his.

A good roast chicken should have lovely crisp brown skin, and the flesh should be moist but well cooked, with no pink bits. I prefer a wing, my kids want skin and breast, and Fergus has it 'as it comes'. In the Canteen, or for events, we roast chickens whole and carve them through the bone, so that you get a lovely juicy piece of meat on the bone.

When buying a chicken, look out for free-range – it is always good to know that your chicken has been running around, looking at the sky.

Serve with roast lemon potatoes (see page 129) and wilted watercress. Cooking the watercress quickly seems to bring out its flavours.

SERVES 4

1 x 1.5kg free-range chicken,
  with giblets (Sutton Hoo are good)
1 bulb of garlic, halved horizontally
  (use one half for the stock)
1 lemon
a small bunch of fresh thyme
2 bay leaves
2 tablespoons olive oil
150g unsalted butter
sea salt and freshly ground black pepper
100ml dry white wine

For the stock
the giblets from the bird

½ a bulb of garlic (see above)
1 stick of celery, chopped
½ an onion, chopped
1 carrot, chopped
1 leek, chopped
2 bay leaves
2 sprigs of fresh thyme
2 sprigs of fresh rosemary

To serve
1 tablespoon olive oil
2 bags of watercress, washed
sea salt and freshly ground black pepper

Take the chicken out of the fridge an hour or half an hour before you want to cook it. To make the stock, put the giblets into a medium-sized pan with half the bulb of garlic, the celery, onion, carrot and leek. Add the herbs, then add water to cover and bring to the boil. Reduce the heat and simmer for 30 minutes, then strain and set aside until needed.

Preheat the oven to 200°C/fan 180°C/400°F/gas 6. Into the chicken's cavity pop the remaining half bulb of garlic, half the lemon and the herbs. Rub the bird with the olive oil and spread the butter all over the skin, squeezing over the juice from the other half lemon. Season really well with salt and pepper.

Place the bird in a roasting tray and roast in the preheated oven for 10 minutes, then turn the oven down to 180°C/fan 160°C/350°F/gas 4 for a further hour. Check that the bird is cooked by spearing the inside of the thickest part of the thigh – if any pinkness appears, carry on cooking. Remove the chicken from the oven and leave to rest for 15 minutes. Prop the bird up on the edge of the roasting tray so that all the juices can run out.

Pour the juices into a small pan, carefully skimming off any fat that rises to the top. Add a splash of white wine, then whisk in the stock and simmer for 5 minutes, continuing to skim off the fat. Check for seasoning and strain into a warmed jug.

When you are ready to serve the chicken, heat a tablespoon of olive oil in a pan and add the watercress. Season with salt and pepper and stir as it wilts. Serve straight away.

Serve the chicken with the gravy, the watercress, bread sauce and the lemon potatoes opposite. New potatoes can also be cooked around the base of the bird at the same time, so that they sup up all the flavours from the chicken. Just add them to the pan at the beginning, sprinkled with salt and a little black pepper.

Lemon Potatoes

I love these potatoes. James, the chef at the Canteen, serves them with roast chicken – delicious. His father, an opera-singing chef, makes them in his restaurant in Halifax. They are unctuous and gently spicy, and the crisp burnt bits on the bottom are what everyone fights over. I have tried replacing the lemon with sumac and it worked very well – probably ruining years of Greek culture.

SERVES 4

1kg Cyprus potatoes
1 teaspoon paprika
500g tomatoes, cut into quarters
4 cloves of garlic, crushed
1 lemon, cut into quarters
70ml olive oil
sea salt and freshly ground black pepper

Preheat the oven to 220°C/fan 200°C/425°F/gas 7.

Peel the potatoes and cut them into halves or quarters, depending on their size. Put them into a roasting tray and add the oil, paprika, tomatoes and crushed garlic. Squeeze over the lemon quarters, then add the lemon skins to the tray. Season with salt and pepper and give it all a big mix. Roast in the preheated oven for 40 minutes, then turn the oven down to 180°C/fan 160°C/350°F/gas 4 for a further 15 minutes.

The potatoes will be ready when they're crispy on the outside and soft when squeezed. When serving, make sure everyone gets some of the crispy bits on the bottom.

DINNER

A lot of my most memorable dinners have been for special occasions: birthdays and children's christenings. Often we just get boxes of langoustines in, or a couple of boxes of asparagus – doing something simple like that so everyone eats the same thing, because we don't have much space. You need to keep it quite straightforward.

At home we've always cooked simply: big pots of things like braised lamb shanks, or fennel sausages with polenta. Stews are always warming and delicious to have simmering on the stove. You are already winning just with the smells. If you make them the day before, the flavours will get better and also you have your hands free for serving drinks and sitting and chatting. It's important to be with your guests, not too busy or too stressed to chat. Look relaxed, even if you're not.

If you're serving a big pot of something that's hard to pass around, put a pile of plates in front of a game guest and get them to serve everyone at their end of the table. It's important to pick the right person to be Mum. Serving is an art: it's about portion control – never overload a plate, otherwise you can be defeated before you start.

Buffets are not my favourite way to eat, but sometimes they work well. It can be an efficient way to serve lots of people in a relaxed fashion. I just hate the buffet queue: it seems a shame to go out for supper and end up queuing, but sometimes it's unavoidable. The nice thing about a buffet is that you can eat at slightly different times – but then you do lose your focus. Sitting down for dinner, you're all in it together. You reach a fever pitch when you sit down to eat – the energy goes up and then it comes down, while a buffet is more meandering. The most important thing with a buffet is that you have to make sure everything can be eaten with a fork.

Eating on your lap is a real bore. Don't invite me for dinner if I'm going to eat on my lap. A table is always a great asset.

Food in small bowls, that you eat standing up, works quite well, and can be passed around or served from one area, almost like an upmarket soup kitchen. Oomphy salads make sense, like the confit duck, lentils and pickled vegetables. It's all there in one dish and easy to eat with a fork. Bakes, like potato and swede, or potato and cep, are good fork eating.

Feeding the masses

Sausages and Parsley Liquor

This dish is dead easy and came my way years ago when the glorious Sarah Lucas cooked for Fergus and me – her mother and grandmother had cooked it for her. As with all recipes, the key to this dish is finding great produce: onions with youth on their side, best picked from the ground if you happen to have a garden – otherwise look for small to medium onions, not too large and flabby; good potatoes; and a fine plain pork sausage, made with good pork.

SERVES 4

800g potatoes (it really just depends
  on how much mash you like)
500g red or white onions
8 thick pork sausages
1 litre cold water
75g butter

150ml milk
2 tablespoons cornflour
a bunch of fresh curly parsley, leaves
  picked and finely chopped
a little malt vinegar

Peel the potatoes and cut them into large chunks. Bring a large pan of salted water to the boil, then add the potatoes and bring back to the boil. Cover the pan and simmer for about 25 minutes, until tender.

Meanwhile, peel the onions and cut into quarters. Layer them with the sausages in a large pan and cover with the water. Bring to the boil, then cover the pan and simmer for 20 minutes.

Drain the potatoes, let them steam dry in the colander for 5 minutes, then mash them with a ricer or potato masher. Add the butter and milk and beat well. Keep warm.

Take the sausages out of the liquor and put them on a plate. When they are cool enough to handle, peel off the skin – a small sharp knife will be helpful here. You will be left with a pile of rather fragile-looking naked sausages – pop them back into the liquor and bring it back to a simmer. Put the cornflour into a bowl and mix it with a little of the liquor from the sausages, making sure there are no lumps. Stir the cornflour mixture into the pan.

Just before serving, stir in the parsley and vinegar. Serve the sausages with piles of buttery mash. The plate will be a joy of gentle colours.

For 10
2kg potatoes
1.2kg red or white onions
20 thick pork sausages
2.5 litres cold water
200g butter
375ml milk
90g cornflour
200g fresh curly parsley, leaves
   picked and finely chopped
a little malt vinegar

For 20
4kg potatoes
2.4kg red or white onions
40 thick pork sausages
5 litres cold water
400g butter
750ml milk
180g cornflour
350g fresh curly parsley, leaves
   picked and finely chopped
a little malt vinegar

For 30
6 kg potatoes
3.6kg red or white onions
60 thick pork sausages
7.5 litres cold water
600g butter
1.2 litres milk
270g cornflour
500g fresh curly parsley, leaves
   picked and finely chopped
a little malt vinegar

Notes on scaling up the recipe:
• Cook the potatoes in batches to fit your biggest pan. Use a potato ricer or, even better, a mouli to mash the larger amounts. The mash can be made a bit in advance, then transferred into large trays or roasting tins, dotted with butter and covered with cling-film and then with foil. Keep in a warming oven for a maximum of 2 hours, until ready to serve. Do not be tempted to let the mash cool and reheat, or it will go lumpy.
• Cook the sausages with the onions and water in batches if necessary, again to fit your largest pan. The sausages, onions and liquor can be made a few hours in advance and reheated. Stir in the parsley and vinegar only when serving.

Braised Fennel Sausages and Polenta

This is one of our family staples – an ordinary dinner becomes a feast, a large platter oozing with polenta and sauce, topped by a pile of sausages.

Italian sausages can be found in most Italian delis and some butcher's shops. They work well roasted and grilled, but slowly, so that they relax and soften.

SERVES 5

4 red onions
4 cloves of garlic
125ml olive oil
2 bulbs of fennel
10 Italian pork and fennel sausages

½ a bottle of red wine
1 x 400g tin of chopped tomatoes
sea salt and freshly ground black pepper
a bundle of fresh herbs, tied together, e.g.
   thyme, parsley, rosemary and bay leaf

Preheat the oven to 160°C/fan 150°C/325°F/gas 3.

Cut the onions into wedges, and peel and thinly slice the garlic. Heat half the olive oil in a frying pan and gently cook the onions and garlic for 5 minutes. Meanwhile cut the fennel into wedges, add to the onions and cook for a further 5 minutes or so.

In a separate pan brown the sausages in the remaining olive oil for about 10 minutes, on a medium heat, turning them often until they have a good all-over colour. Add the red wine and the tinned tomatoes, and bubble away for a few moments.

Arrange the fennel mixture in an ovenproof baking dish (about 32cm diameter, 5cm deep) and add the sausages with their tomato sauce. Season with a little salt and pepper and add the bundle of herbs. Cook in the preheated oven for an hour, then turn the heat up to 190°C/fan 170°C/375°F/gas 5 and cook for a further 10 minutes. The sauce should be rich and the sausages richly browned.

Serve on soft polenta (see page 160), with a rocket salad.

For 10
8 red onions
8 cloves of garlic
200ml olive oil
4 bulbs of fennel
20 Italian pork and fennel sausages
1 bottle of red wine
2 x 400g tins of chopped tomatoes
sea salt and freshly ground black pepper
2 bundles of herbs, tied together, e.g.
    thyme, parsley, rosemary and bay leaf

For 20
16 red onions
16 cloves of garlic
350ml olive oil
8 bulbs of fennel
40 Italian pork and fennel sausages
2 bottles of red wine
4 x 400g tins of chopped tomatoes
sea salt and freshly ground black pepper
4 bundles of herbs, tied together, e.g.
    thyme, parsley, rosemary and bay leaf

For 30
24 red onions
24 cloves of garlic
500ml olive oil
12 bulbs of fennel
60 Italian pork and fennel sausages
3 bottles of red wine
6 x 400g tins of chopped tomatoes
sea salt and freshly ground black pepper
6 bundles of herbs, tied together, e.g.
    thyme, parsley, rosemary and bay leaf

Notes on scaling up the recipe:
• Use boxed red wine for ease and good value, as there is so much needed.
• Brown the sausages in batches, using as many frying pans as possible on the stove.
• Brown the vegetables in a large pan, and give them a longer cooking time,
    approximately 2–3 times longer.
• The sausages, vegetables and reduced wine will need to be assembled in large oven
    trays, with as many ingredients as will fit comfortably in one layer.
• Use the fan setting so that the oven temperature is more evenly spread in the oven,
    and so that different batches can be put on different shelves.
• Allow a longer cooking time for the larger volume of food in the oven – around 1½
    hours, then 20 minutes on the higher temperature. Cook in batches as necessary.

Braised Lamb Shanks and Haricot Beans

SERVES 4

2 tablespoons olive oil
4 lamb shanks, weighing about 500g each
8 shallots
2 bulbs of fennel
2 leeks
6 cloves of garlic

a bundle of fresh herbs, tied together,
  e.g. parsley, sage, thyme and bay leaves
375ml dry white wine
3 x 400g tins of haricot beans, drained
rind of 1 lemon, removed in strips
1 litre chicken stock
sea salt and freshly ground black pepper

Preheat the oven to 180°C/fan 160°C/350°F/gas 4.

Heat the olive oil in a heavy-bottomed ovenproof pan or casserole dish large enough to hold all the lamb shanks and add the shanks two at a time, turning them for about 5 minutes until they are browned all over. Put them on a plate and set aside.

Peel the shallots, leaving them whole, and cut the fennel and leeks into 1.5cm slices. They need to be quite thick so they don't fall apart. Crush the garlic. Add all the vegetables and the tied herbs to the pan or casserole and cook for 15 minutes, turning frequently, so that they become lightly golden. Turn the heat up, add the wine, and reduce for a couple of minutes on a high heat.

Add the beans and lemon rind and pour over the stock. Now return the lamb shanks to the pan, meat side down – the ingredients should all fit quite snugly. Bring to the boil, then cover the dish and slowly braise in the preheated oven for 1½ hours, until the meat is tender. Take the lid off and continue to cook for another 30 minutes to get a nice brown colour on top.

Discard the bundle of herbs and the pieces of lemon rind, check the seasoning, and serve.

For 10

6 tablespoons olive oil

10 lamb shanks, weighing
   about 500g each

20 shallots

5 bulbs of fennel

5 leeks

15 cloves of garlic

2 bundles of fresh herbs, tied together,
   e.g. parsley, sage, thyme and bay leaves

1 litre dry white wine

8 x 400g tins of haricot beans, drained

rind of 3 lemons, removed in strips

2.5 litres chicken stock

sea salt and freshly ground black pepper

For 20

12 tablespoons olive oil

20 lamb shanks, weighing
   about 500g each

40 shallots

10 bulbs of fennel

10 leeks

30 cloves of garlic

4 bundles of fresh herbs, tied together,
   e.g. parsley, sage, thyme and bay leaves

2 litres dry white wine

16 x 400g tins of haricot beans, drained

rind of 6 lemons, removed in strips

5 litres chicken stock

sea salt and freshly ground black pepper

For 30

18 tablespoons olive oil

30 lamb shanks, weighing
   about 500g each

60 shallots

15 bulbs of fennel

15 leeks

45 cloves of garlic

6 bundles of fresh herbs, tied together,
   e.g. parsley, sage, thyme and bay leaves

3 litres dry white wine

22 x 400g tins of haricot beans, drained

rind of 9 lemons, removed in strips

7 litres chicken stock

sea salt and freshly ground black pepper

Notes on scaling up the recipe:
- Brown the lamb shanks in batches, using as many frying pans on the stove as possible.
- Brown the vegetables in a very large pan – all together. Allow longer for this.
- Assemble the ingredients in large deep oven trays or casserole dishes, as large as will comfortably fit into your oven. Cover them tightly with foil.
- Use the fan setting so that the oven temperature is more evenly spread in the oven, and so that different batches can be put on different shelves.
- As there will be a larger mass of ingredients in the oven when cooking in these numbers, the braising time will be longer, anything from 2–3 hours. Keep checking after 2 hours.

Lamb Harira

This is a good hearty stew for feeding the masses. You need to start it the day before.

SERVES 6–8

250g dried chickpeas
750g lamb shoulder or leg
75g fresh ginger, peeled and grated,
  plus 1 teaspoon for finishing
1 tablespoon ground cinnamon
1 tablespoon ground turmeric
1 tablespoon ground paprika
6 cloves of garlic, chopped
2 onions, thinly sliced
2 bay leaves

2 lemons
1 teaspoon baking powder
60ml olive oil
2 glasses of white wine
1 x 400g tin of chopped tomatoes
100g brown or green lentils
sea salt and freshly ground black pepper
a large bunch of fresh coriander
natural yoghurt, to serve

Day 1
Put the chickpeas into a large bowl and cover with cold water. Leave them to soak overnight.

Cut the meat into 2cm pieces, leaving a little fat on but not too much. Put the grated ginger into a bowl with the spices, garlic, onions, bay leaves and the juice of 1 lemon. Add the lamb, mix well, then cover the bowl and leave in the fridge overnight.

Day 2
Drain the chickpeas. Put them into a large pan, cover them with fresh cold water and add the baking powder. Bring to the boil, skimming off the scum. Turn the heat down to low and cook for about an hour, until the chickpeas are really tender. Leave to cool in their liquid, then drain, reserving the cooking water.

Heat the olive oil in a large pan. Add the meat and spices and fry quickly to seal. You may need to do this in batches. Once the pieces are sealed, pour in the wine, cook for a couple of minutes, then add the tinned tomatoes, 250ml of water and 250ml of the reserved chickpea water. Add the lentils and half the cooked chickpeas. Crush the rest of the chickpeas with a fork or whiz in a food processor, and add to the pan. Once the stew has come up to a slight bubble, turn down to a very low heat and simmer for 1½ hours, until the meat is tender.

Leave to cool. If you leave it overnight and reheat it next day, like most stews the flavours get better.

Day 3
Before serving, gently reheat the stew. Squeeze in the juice of the remaining lemon, season with salt and pepper, and add 1 teaspoon of grated ginger and a few handfuls of chopped coriander. Finish with a dollop of yoghurt.

For 10
300g dried chickpeas
1kg lamb shoulder or leg
100g fresh ginger, peeled and grated,
  plus 1½ teaspoons for finishing
1½ tablespoons ground cinnamon
1½ tablespoons ground turmeric
1½ tablespoons ground paprika
8 cloves of garlic, chopped
3 onions, thinly sliced

3 bay leaves
3 lemons
1½ teaspoons baking powder
75ml olive oil
425ml white wine
1 x 400g tin of chopped tomatoes
125g brown or green lentils
sea salt and freshly ground black pepper
40g fresh coriander
natural yoghurt, to serve

For 20

600g dried chickpeas

2kg lamb shoulder or leg

200g fresh ginger, peeled and grated,
   plus 3 teaspoons for finishing

2½ tablespoons ground cinnamon

2½ tablespoons ground turmeric

2½ tablespoons ground paprika

16 cloves of garlic, chopped

5 onions, thinly sliced

6 bay leaves

6 lemons

2½ teaspoons baking powder

150ml olive oil

900ml white wine

3 x 400g tins of chopped tomatoes

250g brown or green lentils

sea salt and freshly ground black pepper

80g fresh coriander

natural yoghurt, to serve

For 30

900g dried chickpeas

3kg lamb shoulder or leg

300g fresh ginger, peeled and grated,
   plus 5 teaspoons for finishing

4 tablespoons ground cinnamon

4 tablespoons ground turmeric

4 tablespoons ground paprika

24 cloves of garlic, chopped

8 onions, thinly sliced

10 bay leaves

9 lemons

4 teaspoons baking powder

225ml olive oil

1.3 litres white wine

4 x 400g tins of chopped tomatoes

375g brown or green lentils

sea salt and freshly ground black pepper

120g fresh coriander

natural yoghurt, to serve

Notes on scaling up the recipe:
- The chickpeas will take longer to bring to the boil in the larger amounts, but should
  take the same time to cook. Make sure you use a very large pan.
- Brown the lamb in batches, using as many frying pans on the stove as possible.
- Use large lidded pans, stockpots or flameproof casserole dishes to cook the stew
  in batches, 10–15 maximum servings in each batch. Or make use of a slow cooker
  (4 hours on high, 8 hours on low).
- As there will be a larger mass of ingredients when cooking in these numbers, the
  braising time will be longer, anything from 2–3 hours. Keep checking after 2 hours.

Squid and Potato Stew

I discovered this dish in Marcella Hazan's brilliant book *Classic Italian Cooking* – she is an inspiration to all cooks. Buy fresh squid of medium size, and ask the fishmonger to clean them if you don't want the messy job. Cleaning squid can be a bore, with the eyes popping out at you and the ink sacs spurting all over the place. But once you start your attack, it can be satisfying.

SERVES 4

1kg squid
1kg waxy new potatoes
125ml olive oil
8 cloves of garlic, chopped
1 teaspoon dried red chilli flakes
a handful of fresh flat-leaf parsley, chopped
175ml white wine
100g tinned chopped tomatoes (¼ of a tin)
100ml water

Clean the squid. Cut the bodies into 1.5cm wide strips and leave the tentacles whole, unless they are very large. Peel the potatoes and cut into 3–4cm chunks.

Heat the olive oil in a wide, heavy-bottomed pan and add the garlic, chilli and parsley. Cook for a couple of minutes, then turn up the heat and add the squid. Once it is sizzling away, add the white wine and let it bubble for a minute to reduce.

Add the tomatoes and potatoes and pour in the water. Turn the heat down and simmer gently with the lid on for about 40 minutes, stirring occasionally, until the potatoes are cooked through.

For 10
2.5kg squid
2.5kg waxy new potatoes
300ml olive oil
20 cloves of garlic, chopped
2½ teaspoons dried red chilli flakes
2 handfuls of fresh flat-leaf
  parsley, chopped
450ml white wine
250g tinned chopped tomatoes
  (just over ½ a tin)
250ml water

For 20
5kg squid
5kg waxy new potatoes
500ml olive oil
40 cloves of garlic, chopped
5 teaspoons dried red chilli flakes
4 handfuls of fresh flat-leaf
  parsley, chopped
900ml white wine
500g tinned chopped tomatoes
  (1¼ tins)
500ml water

For 30
7kg squid
7kg waxy new potatoes
800ml olive oil
60 cloves of garlic, chopped
7 teaspoons dried red chilli flakes
6 handfuls of fresh flat-leaf
  parsley, chopped
1.4 litres white wine
750g tinned chopped tomatoes
  (just under 2 tins)
750ml water

Notes on scaling up the recipe:
- Use the water amount as an approximation, depending on the size of the pan used.
- This recipe will need to be cooked in smallish batches (i.e. half of the 'serves 10' amounts maximum) in a large and wide sauté pan. The cooking time should be the same as for the 'serves 4' original.
- Separate batches can be made, cooled on large trays and kept in the fridge. The different batches can be reheated together in a large casserole or pan – over a gentle heat. Make only a few hours ahead of time, i.e. not the day before.

Venison Stew

SERVES 6–8

1kg venison shoulder, shank
  or neck (a mixture is good)
2 bottles of red wine
6 cloves of garlic, roughly chopped
4 juniper berries
rind of 1 lemon, removed in strips
6 sprigs of fresh thyme
6 bay leaves
a handful of dried porcini mushrooms
sea salt and freshly ground black pepper

100g flour
100ml olive oil
2 onions, roughly diced
2 leeks, diced
1 x 400g tin of chopped tomatoes
500ml chicken stock
a bunch of fresh herbs, tied together,
  e.g. thyme, bay and parsley
450g carrots

Buy the venison boned, but not cut up. Cut it into 3cm pieces, leaving any fat on. Put the red wine, garlic, juniper berries, lemon rind, thyme and bay leaves into a bowl and add the venison. Leave to marinate for 2 days.

Preheat the oven to 160°C/fan 150°C/325°F/gas 3. Put the porcini into a bowl and cover with hot water. Leave to soak for 10 minutes, then drain.

Remove the meat from the marinade and dry it on kitchen paper. Strain the marinade, discarding the flavourings, and set aside. Toss the meat in the seasoned flour, shaking off any extra. Heat most of the oil in a heavy-bottomed ovenproof pan, then add the meat and let it brown over a high heat – small amounts at a time, otherwise the meat will just stew. Once it's all browned, remove it from the pan and leave to one side.

Add a little more olive oil to the pan, then add the onions and cook gently for 5 minutes. Add the leeks and cook for a further 5 minutes, until the vegetables have softened. Stir in the drained porcini, then add the meat, the strained marinade and the tinned tomatoes. Simmer for a few minutes to boil off the alcohol, then add the stock and herbs. Season with salt and pepper, then cover the pan and transfer to the preheated oven for half an hour.

Peel the carrots and cut into 2cm slices. Add them to the pan and cook for a further 1–1½ hours. The meat should be tender but not collapsing. If the sauce is thinner than you would like, remove the meat and vegetables and simmer the sauce for 10–15 minutes over a medium heat until it has reduced and thickened. Then return the meat and vegetables to the pan and leave to cool.

Good reheated the next day. Any leftovers can be used as a pasta sauce.

For 10

1.25kg venison shoulder, shank or neck
  (a mixture is good)
2 bottles of red wine
8 cloves of garlic, roughly chopped
5 juniper berries
rind of 1½ lemons, removed in strips
8 sprigs of fresh thyme
8 bay leaves
2 handfuls of dried porcini
  mushrooms (20g)

sea salt and freshly ground black pepper
125g flour
125ml olive oil
3 onions, roughly diced
3 small leeks, diced
1 x 400g tin of chopped tomatoes
650ml chicken stock
a bunch of fresh herbs, tied together,
  e.g. thyme, bay and parsley
550g carrots

For 20

2.5kg venison shoulder, shank or neck
  (a mixture is good)
4 bottles of red wine
16 cloves of garlic, roughly chopped
10 juniper berries
rind of 3 lemons, removed in strips
16 sprigs of fresh thyme
16 bay leaves
3 big handfuls of dried porcini
  mushrooms (40g)
sea salt and freshly ground black pepper
250g flour
250ml olive oil
6 onions, roughly diced
5 leeks, diced
3 x 400g tins of chopped tomatoes
1.3 litres chicken stock
2 large bunches of fresh herbs, tied
  together, e.g. thyme, bay and parsley
1kg carrots

For 30

3.75kg venison shoulder, shank
  or neck (a mixture is good)
6 bottles of red wine
24 cloves of garlic, roughly chopped
16 juniper berries
rind of 4 lemons, removed in strips
24 sprigs of fresh thyme
24 bay leaves
5 handfuls of dried porcini
  mushrooms (60g)
sea salt and freshly ground black pepper
375g flour
375ml olive oil
9 onions, roughly diced
7 leeks, diced
4 x 400g tins of chopped tomatoes
2.5 litres chicken stock
4 bunches of fresh herbs, tied together,
  e.g. thyme, bay and parsley
1.5kg carrots

Notes on scaling up the recipe:

• Use boxed red wine for ease and good value, as there is so much needed.

• Marinate the venison in very large Tupperware boxes.

• Brown the venison in batches, using as many frying pans on the stove as possible.

• Brown the vegetables in a very large pan – all together. The greater volume of vegetables there is, the longer they will take, so allow for this and go by how they look and feel rather than by timing.

• Assemble the ingredients in large deep oven trays or casserole dishes, as large as will comfortably fit in your oven. Cover them tightly with foil.

• Use the fan setting so that the oven temperature is more evenly spread in the oven, and so that different batches can be put on different shelves.

• As there will be a larger mass of ingredients in the oven when cooking in numbers, the braising time will be longer, anything from 2½ –3½ hours. Keep checking after 1½ hours. If necessary, brown the meat and the vegetables and then cook in batches in the oven, or alternately braise in a large covered pan on the stove or use a slow cooker – or a combination of all these. As long as the meat has become tender, you can reduce the wine sauce – which will take longer the more there is. Reduce it according to taste and consistency. Mix all the various batches together for consistency and taste for seasoning, adjusting as necessary.

Pasta, polenta and risotto

Cabbage and Truffle Spaghetti

This was the first dish Fergus made me. Simple and delightful. People are often snotty about truffle oil and it can be overdone, but if you use a good one and don't put it over everything it can be a cheeky addition. Obviously a fresh truffle would be more exciting.

SERVES 4

sea salt and freshly ground black pepper
1 x 500g packet of dried spaghetti
1 whole Savoy cabbage
2 tablespoons extra virgin olive oil
a hunk of Parmesan cheese, for grating
truffle oil

Bring a large pan of water to the boil and salt it well. Add the pasta – there should be lots of room for it to cook in.

Meanwhile slice the cabbage thinly, discarding the core. A few minutes before the pasta is cooked, add the cabbage to the pan. Stir. Drain. Mix the pasta, cabbage and olive oil together in a large bowl and season with salt and pepper. Serve with a sprinkle of freshly grated Parmesan and a drizzle of truffle oil.

Spaghetti with Bottarga

Bottarga is the dried cured roe from grey mullet – an expensive delicacy from southern Italy. So keep this lip-smacking beautiful food for special occasions. If you have any bottarga left over, rub it with a little olive oil, wrap it in clingfilm and pop it into the fridge.

SERVES 4

3 cloves of garlic
1 red chilli
1 large spring onion
a large bunch of fresh flat-leaf parsley
1 lemon
4 tablespoons olive oil
a 50–70g piece of bottarga
400g dried spaghetti
sea salt and freshly ground black pepper

Peel and grate the garlic. Finely chop the chilli but discard the seeds. Slice the spring onion finely. Pick, wash, drain and coarsely chop the parsley leaves. Finely grate a teaspoon of the lemon zest.

Heat the olive oil on a low heat. Add the garlic, chilli and spring onion and cook for a few minutes, until softened. Add the parsley and lemon zest and leave to one side.

Grate the bottarga – the more bottarga the better. Leave a little for grating over the top of the pasta.

Cook the pasta in plenty of salted boiling water according to the packet instructions. Drain, leaving it a little wet. Put the pasta back into the pan and toss with the garlicky oil and the grated bottarga. Season with salt and pepper.

Serve the pasta and grate a little more bottarga over each serving.

Tomato and Porcini Pasta

My children are half tomato pasta. This recipe comes from their grandmother Elizabeth, and sometimes they will say, 'Well, Mum, it was good, but not quite as good as Elizabeth's.' Ah well – I do try for the little darlings. The trick, I think, as with all pasta, is to give it lots of love and make sure you don't overcook the pasta.

SERVES 4

2 small onions
4 cloves of garlic
a handful of dried porcini mushrooms
100ml olive oil, plus extra for the pasta
100g unsmoked streaky bacon

2 x 400g tins of whole plum tomatoes
sea salt and freshly ground black pepper
a knob of butter
500g dried spaghetti
1 x 200g block of Parmesan, for grating

Peel the onions and garlic and slice them thinly, keeping them separate. Put the porcini into a small bowl, cover with 140ml of boiling water, and leave to soak.

Heat the oil in a heavy-bottomed pan and cook the onions gently for about 20 minutes, until soft and translucent. Cut the bacon into small pieces and add to the pan with the garlic. Cook for about 12 minutes, until the bacon is done.

Drain the porcini, reserving the liquid. Add the soaked porcini to the pan and cook for 10 minutes. Add the tinned tomatoes and turn the heat up under the pan. Once bubbling, strain the porcini soaking liquid through a fine sieve to get rid of any grit and add to the pan. Turn down the heat and cook for 40 minutes, until the sauce has come together and is rich and lovely. Finish it off with salt, pepper and a knob of butter.

Bring a large pan of water to the boil – always boil lots of water to cook the pasta in, as it needs room to breathe while it cooks. Add the pasta to the pan and cook according to the instructions on the packet. Drain and toss with olive oil. Put the pasta back into the pan and stir in the tomato sauce. Tongs are essential for this.

Serve at the table: lift a tong full twist, turn and gently place on the plate. Pass the hunk of Parmesan around with a grater – it's fun to have everyone grating their own Parmesan. I prefer the fine grate.

Clam, Parsley and Garlic Spaghetti

SERVES 4 AS A MAIN, 6 AS A STARTER

1kg palourdes clams or any clams that are not too large
sea salt and freshly ground black pepper
1 x 500g packet of dried spaghetti
70ml olive oil, plus a little extra for the pasta
6 cloves of garlic, finely chopped
100ml dry white wine
a bunch of fresh flat-leaf parsley, leaves picked
25g butter

A few hours before making this pasta, run the clams under cold water. You may find the shells are dirty; if so, give them a good scrub. Otherwise it will be grit pasta rather than clam pasta.

Bring a large pan of salted water to the boil. Add the pasta and cook according to the packet directions, then drain and toss in a little olive oil.

While this is happening, heat the olive oil in a pan large enough to hold all the clams. Add the garlic and cook on a low heat for approximately 4 minutes. Try not to let it get any colour. Add the white wine, then turn the heat up under the pan and simmer for a few moments. Add the clams, then pop a lid on the pan and wait for them to open. Two minutes should be enough – shake the pan occasionally.

Finely chop the parsley and add to the clams. Stir, add a blob of butter, then stir again. Add the drained spaghetti and stir it all together. Taste, and season with salt and pepper.

Serve in bowls, with lots of wine.

Linguine Carbonara

SERVES 2

6 shallots
1 stick of celery
4 cloves of garlic
100g extra virgin olive oil
a 150g piece of pancetta
150g Parmesan cheese
sea salt and freshly ground black pepper
250g dried linguine
2 eggs
250g crème fraîche

Peel the shallots and slice lengthways into quarters. Cut the celery into the thinnest slices. Slice the garlic. Heat the olive oil in a heavy-bottomed pan and add the shallots, celery and garlic. Cook for a few moments on a gentle heat. Meanwhile, cut the pancetta into small cubes and add to the shallot mixture. Cook gently for 15 minutes. Grate the Parmesan and leave to one side.

Bring a large pan of water to the boil. Add a tablespoon of salt and then the linguine, following the instructions on the packet and not making it too al dente. Drain, reserving a mugful of the pasta water.

In a separate bowl whisk the 2 eggs and mix in the crème fraîche. Pour the crème fraîche and eggs into the shallot mixture and stir on a very low heat for 3 to 4 minutes. Add the Parmesan and a small ladle of pasta water. Add the drained linguine while still hot. Season with black pepper, but check before adding salt as the pancetta will season the mixture.

Pizzoccheri

This is definitely mountain food, though we often eat it at home in London. It's best eaten on a cold day, or midway through an eight-hour hike. It is a combination of many soothing ingredients: pizzoccheri, a traditional buckwheat pasta, which has that lovely gritty texture against your teeth, potatoes, butter and cheeses.

SERVES 6

250g butter, cubed
8 cloves of garlic, finely chopped
600g waxy potatoes
1 medium Savoy cabbage
250g Taleggio cheese
200g Fontina cheese
200g Parmesan cheese
sea salt and freshly ground black pepper
1 x 500g pack of pizzoccheri della Vatellina (from specialist Italian delis)

Heat the butter in a small pan. Add the garlic and cook until soft. Set aside and keep warm.

Bring 2 large pans of water to the boil. Peel and slice the potatoes into happy chunks. Cut the cabbage into thin slices, discarding the core. Cut the Taleggio and Fontina into small chunks, discarding any rind, and finely grate the Parmesan. Have everything ready in separate bowls.

Once the water is boiling, add salt to one pan and cook the potatoes first, as they will take the longest. Remove them from the pan with a slotted spoon and leave to one side. Add salt to the other pan and cook the pizzoccheri for about 8–10 minutes – they should still have a little bite. Drain. Lastly, blanch the cabbage for a couple of minutes in the pan you cooked the pasta in, and drain.

While all the ingredients are still hot, prepare the dish by layering all your ingredients: a layer of pasta, followed by potatoes, cabbage and cheeses. Finally drizzle over the hot garlicky butter, season with salt and pepper, and stir.

Polenta

There are all sorts of different types of polenta. I always follow the packet instructions. Some are quick to cook and some types take a very long time. All are good for your arm muscles, as cooking polenta involves a lot of stirring. I prefer the long-cooking type, as it makes for a good meditative moment.

Soft polenta

SERVES 6

1 litre milk
1 litre water
500g coarse white polenta
sea salt and freshly ground black pepper
100g butter, diced
200g Parmesan cheese, grated

Heat the milk and water in a large heavy-bottomed pan. When it's simmering, add the polenta in a slow stream, whisking constantly to avoid lumps. Change to a wooden spoon and continue to stir for 40–45 minutes on a low heat.

When the polenta comes away from the sides of the pan easily it is cooked. Season with salt and pepper and finally stir in the butter and Parmesan.

Serve straight on to the plates. Wet polenta is lovely with grilled radicchio, and a rich tomato sauce (see page 154).

Polenta to grill or fry

SERVES 4

1 litre water
250g coarse yellow polenta
sea salt and freshly ground black pepper
30g butter, diced
50g Parmesan cheese, grated
light olive oil, for frying (e.g. Olivetti)

Make the polenta as opposite, or follow the packet instructions if using instant polenta, then pour into a lightly oiled container and spread out flat. Once cold, cut into wedges.

Put at least 10cm of light olive oil into a deep pan and heat to 120°C. Fry the polenta in batches for about 4–5 minutes, until crispy. Serve with a tomato sauce on the side, like chips and ketchup.

For grilling, brush the polenta with oil and grill on the barbecue or indoor grill. Grill on both sides, for several minutes – leave it long enough for the polenta not to stick. Once crisp it will be easier to slide a spatula underneath, turn it over and crisp the other side. Patience is needed here. Serve with a tomato salad.

Porcini and Cavolo Nero Risotto

Risottos are wonderful dishes, taking on all the surrounding flavours. Cooking a risotto is definitely something you need to practise, as the more you know your rice the better the flavour and texture will be. A one-pot wonder is always good for large groups, but it can be difficult cooking too much risotto in one pot, so sometimes it's better to have a couple of separate pots cooking.

SERVES 4

50g dried porcini mushrooms
1.5 litres vegetable stock
  (stock cubes are fine)
2 red onions
2 tablespoons olive oil
a couple of blobs of butter
4 cloves of garlic, chopped

200g cavolo nero
200g risotto rice
100ml white wine
sea salt and freshly ground black pepper
150g Parmesan, grated, plus more for
  serving if required

Put the porcini into a bowl and cover with boiling water. Leave to soak. Bring the stock to a simmer, then keep it warm until you need it.

Peel the red onions and cut into thin slivers. Heat the olive oil and a blob of butter in a pan and sauté the red onions slowly until they soften. Add the garlic. Rip the cavolo nero leaves from the central stalk and slice into thin strips. Discard the stalk. Add the leaves to the onions and sauté until softened.

Drain the porcini and add to the pan. Cook for 2 minutes, then add the rice, stirring until it is hot. Add the wine, then turn the heat up and reduce it by a third. Season with salt and pepper.

Turn the heat down to low and add the hot stock to the rice a ladleful at a time, stirring while each ladleful is absorbed before adding the next. Taste and season. Once the rice is cooked but still has a little bite (after about 20 minutes), add the grated Parmesan and a big blob of butter. Stir – it should be creamy but not claggy, and each piece of rice should have its own identity. Leave the risotto to settle for a few moments.

Serve with extra Parmesan, for those who want more.

CELEBRATORY DINNERS

Celebratory meals can be more nerve-racking than a usual supper party, so what makes a special dinner special, and how do you get the festivities going?

The guests are very important: bringing generous-spirited friends and family together has always been a passion. I always try to visualize them while I plan a meal: what would they like to eat, what are their needs, do they drink, are they vegetarian? Otherwise, the season helps to decide the menu, generally.

To make things festive, it is essential to think about flowers and tablecloths. Clean the cutlery and buy new candles. If it's an extra-special occasion, iron the napkins. Sometimes for family weddings or anniversaries we've had aprons embroidered with dates and initials – something people can keep for a happy memory.

Start with a cocktail, it lifts the spirits and creates excitement, a bit of theatre and glamour to bring laughter and conversation. Lots of treats are what one wants for celebratory dinners. I am a big believer in piles of things: langoustines, asparagus, salads, birds. But mostly guests are happy with simple food, wonderfully cooked. A beautifully roasted chicken can make your guests as happy as a whole brill. Always try to use young fresh vegetables, and animals from good farms that have eaten well and lived good lives.

I hate not being able to hear what is being said because there is murmuring background noise, so best to keep music for dancing after dinner.

Dinners can be quite tiring, so a little digestif works well to get everyone going again.

Something to start with

Whitebait, Lemon and Sage

Ayliffe Maddever, the brilliant chef who once ran the wonderful and delicious restaurant Java, cooked me this last time I was in New Zealand. Luckily for me I happened to be there in whitebait season. Whitebait in New Zealand is special and can't be found here in the UK. Elvers are the same as New Zealand whitebait, tiny morsels with no bone structure – an expensive delicacy. They make an excellent fritter as well.

SERVES 4

a dollop of butter
2 fresh sage leaves
500g frozen whitebait (from Chinatown, in the freezer,
  or fresh if you are in the right part of the world)
sea salt and freshly ground black pepper
1 lemon

Melt the butter in a heavy-bottomed frying pan. Add the sage leaves and sizzle for a moment. Take out the leaves and add the whitebait. Cook quickly at a reasonable heat, tossing and seasoning with salt and pepper as you go, but don't burn the butter. These little, translucent, worm-like fish will take literally 2 minutes.
    Serve at once, with lemon wedges and a green salad.

Artichoke Vinaigrette

Artichokes are always wonderful to serve: they look so good standing proudly on the plate, and their gentle flavour seems designed to sup up vinaigrette. I remember my first artichoke, when I skived off school to have lunch with my mother at Plimmer Steps: sprinting down to meet her, ordering this glorious thistle and learning the sucking technique. Then the treat at the bottom: it's so satisfying to push the choke off with your thumb to reveal the heart. In Venice the stallholders cut away the leaves and just sell the beautiful hearts. They sit in baths of lemony water, waiting to be braised or fried.

SERVES 6

6 globe artichokes
2 lemons, sliced
1 bulb of garlic, halved
sea salt

Prepare the artichokes by snapping off the stalks – just grab them near the base and pull back, with a firm hand. This will help pull out some of the stringy bits. Snap off some of the outer leaves if they don't look too happy, otherwise leave them as they are.

   Put the artichokes into a large stainless steel pan and cover with plenty of water. Add the lemons, garlic and a pinch of salt. Bring up to the boil and cook for about 40 minutes, until the base is soft when you pierce it and the leaves are easy to pull out.

   Carefully take the artichokes out of the water and leave them upside down to cool. Trim the bottom of each artichoke so it sits flat on the plate. Serve with a bowl of mustard vinaigrette on the side.

Asparagus

Spring is here at last and my birthday is not far away. I love that moment, the big change happening, and the prospect of green stalky vegetables, lots of shoots and wonderful British asparagus.

I don't peel – maybe it's my brown bread upbringing but I never have a problem with the outer skin of the asparagus. You can snap the ends off, but this often makes them too short, so I slice off the stalky ends with a sharp knife. If you are serving asparagus as a pass-around canapé, you can make them just a bit shorter (easier to eat if you're standing up). The stalks can be used for vegetable stock or soup.

Asparagus and Butter (SERVES 6)

36 asparagus spears, trimmed
100g unsalted butter, melted
sea salt and freshly ground black pepper

Bring a decent-sized pan of water to the boil and add salt. Once you have a rolling boil, blanch the asparagus for 3½–4 minutes, depending on their size. Serve with melted butter, salt and pepper.

Lemon and Olive Oil Dressing (SERVES 6)

60ml lemon juice (about 2 lemons)
100ml olive oil
sea salt and freshly ground black pepper

Squeeze the lemon juice into a bowl and add the olive oil. Season with salt and pepper and pour over the tips of your freshly blanched asparagus spears. Try to leave the ends dressing-free, so they can be picked up easily, without fingers getting too mucky. A soft-boiled egg goes well with this.

Hollandaise Sauce (SERVES 6)

250g butter
3 egg yolks
60ml reduction (see below)
juice of ½ a lemon
sea salt and freshly ground black pepper

For the reduction
250ml dry white wine
1 teaspoon whole black peppercorns
1 bay leaf
1 large shallot, sliced

To make the reduction, put the wine, peppercorns, bay leaf and shallot into a small pan and reduce over a high heat for 5 minutes, until you have 60ml left. Strain and leave to cool slightly.

Now for the hollandaise: slowly melt the butter in a small pan and keep it warm.

Put the egg yolks into a metal or glass bowl, add the reduction, and place the bowl over a pan of barely simmering water – the bowl should fit snugly on top. Whisk the egg yolks and reduction with a balloon whisk until frothy and quite stiff. It takes about 10 minutes, but feel your way and make sure the heat is gentle, as you don't want to end up with scrambled eggs. Take the egg yolk mix off the heat.

You may need someone to help with the next bit, or you can stand the bowl on a damp cloth, which will keep it grounded. Slowly, slowly pour the warm butter in, whisking all the time – a squeeze of lemon may help this to come together. A tiny bit of hot water will also loosen the mix so you can pour more butter in.

Once all the butter has been added, season with salt and pepper and maybe add another squeeze of lemon. Keep it warm – a Thermos is good for this, especially if you need to transport it somewhere.

Serve with piles of your freshly blanched asparagus.

Langoustines and Mayonnaise

Simple but expensive. Buy them alive and kicking. Check them over, to make sure they are alive and a good colour. I prefer the medium or small ones, as they are easier for your guests to shell. Don't be afraid of your guests doing the shelling – my kids could shell a langoustine and suck the head almost at the same time they began to walk. Ah, that's a proud mother speaking.

You need at least six langoustines per person, though most people can eat more. Cook them as soon as possible. Even if you are eating them the next day, they need to be cooked as soon as you can.

Bring some water to the boil in a pan large enough to fit the langoustines comfortably. Salt the water, and when you have a gentle rolling boil add the langoustines whole. Don't cram them in. Cook them for 2 minutes. If the tails flick back, you know they're cooked. Take them out of the pan with tongs or a spider and leave them on a tray to cool.

Keep them in the fridge if you aren't eating them until the next day, but take them out an hour before you need them so they aren't too cold.

For the mayonnaise (makes 550g)
3 egg yolks
1 teaspoon Dijon mustard
juice of 1 lemon
450ml olive oil
sea salt and freshly ground black pepper

Put the egg yolks, mustard and half the lemon juice into a bowl or a food processor (I prefer the processor). Whiz together, then with the machine running, slowly add the olive oil through the funnel. If you are using a bowl, place it on a damp tea towel to keep it grounded. Whisk the egg yolks, mustard and lemon juice together, then slowly, slowly add the olive oil, whisking all the time.

As the mixture thickens, you can add the oil a little faster. Add the rest of the lemon juice – this will thin it down, making it easier to add the oil. A tablespoon of boiling water will thin the mayo down a little further if you don't want it too thick. When it's ready, season it with salt and pepper. (If the mayonnaise splits, whisk up another egg yolk and whisk it into the split mixture at the slowest pace possible.)

Serve the langoustines lined up like soldiers, on a beautiful platter. Surround them with bowls of mayo and lemon halves, with baskets of crusty bread. A few fingerbowls scattered about are always handy. A feast fit for a wedding.

Main courses

Veal Shin and Fennel

SERVES 4

12 shallots
8 cloves of garlic
3 tablespoons olive oil
1 whole veal shin, weighing about 2.5kg
sea salt and freshly ground black pepper
200ml white wine
750ml chicken stock
6 bulbs of fennel
a bunch of fresh herbs, tied together,
   e.g. fennel, thyme, rosemary and bay leaves

Preheat the oven to 170°C/fan 150°C/325°F/gas 3.

Peel the shallots and garlic, keeping both whole. Heat the olive oil in a pan, then season the veal shin with salt and pepper and brown it all over in the oil. Remove from the pan, add the shallots and garlic and cook until golden. Pour in the wine and reduce a little, then add the stock and bring to the boil. Keep warm on a low heat.

Cut each fennel bulb into wedges. Put the veal shin into a roasting pan large enough to hold all the ingredients, add the fennel, and pour over the hot shallot stock. Add the bunch of herbs and season with salt and pepper, then cover with foil and cook in the preheated oven for 3½ hours.

When ready, skim any fat off the top and serve with new potatoes or polenta (see page 160). This is also delicious cold, as it makes a wonderful jelly, but be sure to skim all the fat off.

Baked Whole Brill

Brill is a glamorous flatfish with firm white flesh. It is a treat to cook, as it holds itself beautifully. A crowd-pleaser – it's hard to find someone who doesn't like brill. It's so pleasing to cook a fish whole, tastier for a start, and fun to eat the cheeks, pick the frame clean and proudly hold the cleaned skeleton and know there has been no wastage.

SERVES 4–6

1 whole brill, weighing about 2–3kg
50ml olive oil
sea salt and freshly ground black pepper
75g butter
1 lemon

Ask your fishmonger to scale and gut the fish.

Preheat the oven to 200°C/fan 180°C/400°F/gas 6.

Wash the fish and pat it dry, making sure the cavity is clean. Brush it with olive oil and season with salt and pepper.

Heat an oven tray that is big enough to hold the fish and will fit in your oven, and, once hot, drizzle with a little olive oil. Place the fish on the pan and blob a few bits of butter over it. Squeeze over half the lemon and bake for 10 minutes. Turn the grill on and finish by browning the fish for 2 minutes.

Serve with braised fennel or new potatoes, just to be a bit old school.

Baked Halibut with Capers and Lemon

SERVES 4

4 pieces of halibut, cut on the bone (tranches)
sea salt and freshly ground black pepper
olive oil
2 tablespoons butter
a splash of white wine
juice of ½ a lemon
1 tablespoon capers

Preheat the oven to 180°C/fan 160°C/350°F/gas 4.

Season the fish with salt and pepper, then brush an ovenproof pan with olive oil and place it over a medium heat. Add half the butter and a little olive oil to the pan and when it's sizzling, slide in the fish. Brown it on one side, then turn it over and place the pan in the preheated oven. Cook for 7 minutes. Check if it is done by pressing the flesh: it is ready when it gently comes away from the bone.

Take the fish out of the pan and place it to one side. Add a splash of wine to the pan and return it to the heat, letting it bubble away until the wine has reduced. Pop in the lemon juice and capers, stir in the rest of the butter, and shuggle the pan so that all the ingredients come together. Taste and season the sauce, then pour over the fish.

Serve with potatoes and chard.

Slow-roast Leg of Lamb with Cracked Wheat

SERVES 6

1 leg of lamb on the bone, weighing about 1.8–2kg
2 tablespoons olive oil
sea salt and freshly ground black pepper
8 cloves of garlic
10 shallots
4 ripe tomatoes
a bunch of fresh rosemary, thyme and bay leaves
rind of 1 lemon, removed in strips
375ml white wine
200ml dry vermouth
250g bulgar wheat

Take the lamb out of the fridge an hour or two before you want to cook it, to bring it to room temperature. Preheat the oven to 120°C/fan 110°C/250°F/gas ½.

Heat the oil in a frying pan or casserole large enough to hold the lamb. Season the leg with salt and pepper and brown it all over in the oil. Peel the garlic and shallots, cut the tomatoes in half, and tie the herbs into a bundle. Put all of these into a large roasting tray with the lemon rind, and put the lamb in the centre. Pour over the wine and vermouth. Season well with salt and pepper, then cover with foil.

Cook for 6 hours, checking occasionally – if there are not enough juices, add a little water. Add the bulgar wheat and cook for another hour. When the lamb is done, remove it to a board, then check the bulgar wheat for seasoning and spoon it on to a flat serving dish with the vegetables. Place the lamb on top, and serve in slices (it should come away easily from the bone) with lightly steamed sprout tops, spring greens or cabbage.

Roast Rack of Lamb

SERVES 4–5

2 racks of lamb, weighing about 650g each
  (approx. 7 cutlets per rack)
sea salt and freshly ground black pepper
1 tablespoon olive oil

Take the racks out of the fridge and leave for half an hour so they can come to room temperature. Then preheat the oven to 180°C/fan 160°C/350°F/gas 4.

Season the racks all over with salt and pepper. Heat the oil in a heavy-bottomed ovenproof pan, and once it comes to a medium heat, put the racks in with the fat side facing down and brown gently for a few minutes, rendering some of the fat down. Pour the fat off and put the pan into the oven, leaving the rack fat side down, for 15 minutes, or until the tip of a slim, sharp knife comes out warm to your lip when you spear the meat. Or, if using a temperature gauge, when it reads 50°C (for medium rare). Leave to rest on a board, covered loosely with foil, for at least 15 minutes.

Carve the cutlets and pile them up in a bowl. Serve with green sauce (see page 302), new potatoes and roast beetroot.

Tip: If this is all making a crazy amount of smoke in the kitchen and fire alarms are going off, you can change tack. Heat the heavy-bottomed pan in the oven at 200°C/fan 180°C/400°F/gas 6, and put the rack in fat side down (you don't need the oil for this method) for 5 minutes. Then turn the oven down to 180°C/fan 160°C/350°F/gas 4 and cook as above.

Braised Partridge, Potatoes and Pine Nuts

SERVES 4

60ml olive oil
4 partridges
sea salt and freshly ground black pepper
2 onions, sliced
2 sticks of celery, chopped
100g pancetta, cut into chunks
12 cloves of garlic, left whole
60ml sherry vinegar
120ml dry white wine

120ml water
a pinch of saffron
4 bay leaves
2 cloves
a small handful of pine nuts
600g firm potatoes or new potatoes
4 stems of curly kale
a large knob of butter
60g fresh curly parsley, finely chopped

Preheat the oven to 180°C/fan 160°C/350°F/gas 4.

In a heavy-bottomed pan or large lidded casserole dish that the birds will fit into snugly, heat half the oil. Season the birds with salt and pepper and brown them all over, working in batches. Remove from the pan and leave to one side.

Add the onions and celery to the pan and cook for about 5 minutes, until softened. Add the pancetta and cook for another 5 minutes, until browned. Add the whole cloves of garlic and soften slowly. Add the vinegar, wine, water, saffron, bay leaves, cloves and pine nuts. Put the birds back into the pan, surrounded by the unctuous base. Bring the liquid to the boil, then reduce the heat, cover the pan and cook for 1 hour, by which time the birds should be tender.

Cut the potatoes into large chunks, add to the pan and cook for a further 30 minutes, or until they are cooked through. Pull the leaves off the kale stems and slice them extra finely, then add them to the pan and stir in. Once they have softened, add a knob of butter and the finely chopped parsley.

Serve one bird, surrounded with the juices and vegetables, to each person.

Rolled Pork Belly, Fennel and Coriander

Jeremy Lee is a wonderful chef and a fantastic host. His meals are always generous and full of all things delicious. This pork dish came after platters of cured salmon and cucumber salad. It can be served straight away, or later at room temperature, or even the next day. So handy if you're cooking for a large group. You could cook a couple of bellies and serve them cold. Lovely with roasted root vegetables.

SERVES 10–12

1 piece of pork belly,
  weighing about 3kg
3 tablespoons fennel seeds
2 tablespoons coriander seeds
6 cloves of garlic
zest of 2 lemons

2 tablespoons fresh thyme leaves
2 large red onions
50ml olive oil
200ml red wine
freshly ground black pepper
2 tablespoons sea salt

Ask your butcher to score the skin of the pork belly and take out the bones. Lay the pork out flat on a board, meat side up, and trim away any loose bits of fat.

Grind the seeds in a mortar with the garlic, lemon zest and thyme leaves.

Peel the onions and slice them thinly. Heat the olive oil in a frying pan, then add the onions and cook them gently for about 20–25 minutes, until soft. Add the red wine, turn up the heat under the pan and cook until the wine has reduced by about three-quarters. Stir in the ground spice mixture and season with pepper.

Preheat the oven to 220°C/fan 200°C/425°F/gas 7. Spread the onion mixture over the pork belly, then roll it up lengthways into a long sausage shape. Using butcher's string, tie the rolled joint in several places, as firmly and evenly as possible. Rub the sea salt into the scored skin.

Put the rolled pork belly into a large roasting tray and cook for 30 minutes, turning it once. The skin will bubble up a bit – this will help it to crisp. Now turn the oven down to 180°C/fan 160°C/350°F/gas 4 and cook the pork for a further 2 hours, turning it every 20 minutes or so. Leave it to rest for at least 20 minutes before untying the string, then carve into slices and serve.

Pan-fried Calves' Liver and Radicchio

SERVES 4

1 tablespoon olive oil
30g unsalted butter
4 pieces of calves' liver, weighing about 150g each
sea salt and freshly ground black pepper
1 tablespoon balsamic vinegar
1 head of radicchio, cut into 12 wedges
125ml chicken stock

Heat the oil and two-thirds of the butter in a large heavy-bottomed frying pan. Season the liver on both sides with salt and pepper. Slide the liver into the pan and fry for 3 minutes, until it has a lovely caramelized colour. Turn and do the same to the other side. The liver should feel firmish, with a little give. Remove it from the pan and set it aside to rest for a moment.

Return the pan to the heat and deglaze with the balsamic vinegar. Add the radicchio and cook, turning occasionally, until it starts to wilt. Pour in the chicken stock, then turn up the heat and cook for a few moments, to reduce. Add the rest of the butter, season with salt and pepper, then shuggle the pan and stir the sauce so it comes together, checking your seasoning again.

Place the radicchio on a platter, lay the liver on top, and finish by pouring over the sauce. Serve with lentils and mustard.

Confit Duck, Lentil and Pickled Vegetable Salad

When my kids were tiny and we were eating our way through Melbourne and Sydney – great restaurants with fantastic food – I can remember loving this salad. You need to start making the confit duck legs the day before you need them.

SERVES 4–6

For the salad
125g Puy lentils
juice of ½ a lemon
1 tablespoon olive oil
sea salt and freshly ground black pepper
½ a handful of capers, drained
a handful of rocket or
  baby spinach leaves
a small handful of fresh mint leaves,
  roughly chopped
1 tablespoon roughly chopped
  fresh flat-leaf parsley
1 tablespoon vinaigrette (see page 73)

For the confit duck legs
2 duck legs
50g sea salt
1 teaspoon freshly ground black pepper
6 sprigs of fresh thyme
6 cloves of garlic, peeled and crushed
500g duck or goose fat

For the pickled vegetables
1 large carrot, peeled,
  then peeled into ribbons
¼ of a cucumber, skin on,
  peeled into ribbons
1 bulb of fennel, cut into very thin slices
10 radishes, trimmed and halved

For the pickling brine
200ml water
150ml white wine vinegar
50g caster sugar
rind of 1 lemon, removed in strips
a piece of fresh ginger
4 cloves
a pinch of ground allspice
1 teaspoon black peppercorns
1 tablespoon sea salt
1 clove of garlic
1 whole fresh red chilli

First make the confit duck legs. Place the duck legs in a plastic container, fleshy side up. Mix the salt and pepper in a little bowl and rub the mixture all over them, then cover and refrigerate overnight.

The next day, remove the duck legs from the fridge, wash off the salt and pepper mixture and pat dry with kitchen paper. Preheat the oven to 110°C/fan 100°C/225°F/gas ¼.

Place the duck legs in an ovenproof dish so that they fit snugly and add the thyme and garlic. Melt the duck fat in a small pan and pour over the duck legs, covering them completely. Cook in the preheated oven for 2½ hours. The meat should be very tender and almost collapsing. Leave to cool completely, then remove the legs from the fat and put them into the fridge while you cook the lentils. Strain the fat, discarding the thyme and garlic, and refrigerate for later use.

Place the lentils in a large pan and cover with cold water. Add the lemon juice and olive oil and bring to the boil. Simmer for 20–25 minutes, until the lentils are cooked, then drain, season and leave to one side to cool.

Meanwhile make the pickled vegetables. Put all the pickling brine ingredients into a large pan and bring to the boil. Reduce the heat and simmer for 15 minutes then set aside and leave to cool. Put the prepared vegetables into a bowl and strain over the cooled pickling brine – the vegetables should be covered. Leave for 20–30 minutes – you want the vegetables to still have a crunch when they are mixed into the salad.

Preheat the oven to 200°C/fan 180°C /400°F/gas 6. Take the duck legs out of the fridge and put them into a frying pan. Heat them, skin side up, for approximately 14 minutes, then take them out of the pan. Remove the skin and set it aside, then take the duck meat off the bone with a fork, trying to keep the pieces of meat a reasonable size, not too shreddy. Place the duck skin on a small baking tray, sprinkle with salt and cook in the preheated oven for 15 minutes, until crisp.

Put the lentils into a decent-sized bowl with the drained pickled vegetables, the capers, leaves and chopped herbs. Add a couple of splashes of vinaigrette, and finally add the duck. Serve in a gracious bowl, with the crisp skin sliced thinly and sprinkled on top.

Vegetables

Potato, Cep and Onion Bake

SERVES 6

2kg new potatoes
6 ceps
6 cloves of garlic
1 lemon
a bunch of fresh flat-leaf parsley
2 onions
150ml olive oil
3 bay leaves
sea salt and freshly ground black pepper

Preheat the oven to 180°C/fan 160°C/350°F/gas 4.

Peel the potatoes and leave them in a pan of water. Slice the ceps into 0.5cm pieces. Peel and chop the garlic, and squeeze the lemon juice. Pick the parsley leaves and chop finely.

Peel the onions and slice thinly. Heat the olive oil in a frying pan and cook the onions and garlic together until softened.

While the onions are cooking, use a mandoline or a sharp knife to slice the potatoes thinly. Put them into a bowl and add the softened onions and garlic, bay leaves, lemon juice and finely chopped parsley. Season with salt and pepper.

Spread a layer of potatoes and onions in a baking dish and arrange the ceps on top, followed by the rest of the potatoes. Cover with foil. Bake in the preheated oven for 1½ hours, until the potatoes are soft, then take the foil off and bake for a bit longer, until the potatoes are brown on top.

Red Cabbage Pickle

MAKES 1.2KG

350ml white wine vinegar
200ml rice wine vinegar
50g caster sugar
1 stick of cinnamon
a 5cm piece of fresh ginger, peeled and bruised
50g yellow mustard seeds
a few black peppercorns
2 cloves
3 bay leaves
1 red chilli
1 red cabbage, weighing about 1kg
2 tablespoons sea salt

Put all the ingredients except the cabbage and salt into a large pan and bring to a simmer. Simmer for 20 minutes, then strain the liquid and leave to cool.

Shred the cabbage finely. Put into a bowl and sprinkle with the salt. Mix well, then leave at room temperature for 24 hours. Rinse the cabbage in cold water and drain, then pack into large sterilized jars and pour over the pickling liquid. Leave for at least 48 hours before eating – it should be crisp, so is best served within the week, otherwise it becomes soft.

Fried Savoy Cabbage, Garlic, Parsley and Chilli

Recently I have discovered a brilliant mix of dried parsley, chilli and garlic, sold in packets in Italian shops, which is very handy when you are about to rustle up something and the cupboard is bare. Alternatively, you can of course use fresh herbs.

SERVES 4

2 handfuls of fresh flat-leaf parsley, chopped
5 cloves of garlic, chopped or grated
1 teaspoon dried chilli (optional)
2 tablespoons olive oil
1 Savoy cabbage, sliced thinly
100ml dry white wine
sea salt and freshly ground black pepper

Put the parsley, garlic and chilli into a stainless pan and add the olive oil. Place over a low heat and fry gently for 3–4 minutes, then add the sliced cabbage. Watch the heat, turning it up or down as needed and stirring every so often.

Add the wine and 100ml of water and put a lid on the pan. Cook on a medium heat for 5 minutes to steam the cabbage, then remove the lid and continue to cook for a further 30–35 minutes on a low heat, until the cabbage is very tender. If you need a little more moisture, add a splash of white wine or water. Season with salt and pepper and serve with meat dishes.

Celeriac Mash

SERVES 8

3 celeriac
400g potatoes
300ml milk
300ml cream
200g butter
sea salt and freshly ground black pepper

Peel the celeriac and potatoes and cut into even hunks. Put the celeriac into a large pan, cover with water and bring to the boil. Once boiling, add the potatoes and cook until both vegetables are tender. Drain, then mash with a mouli or by hand. Heat the milk, cream and butter in a small pan and stir into the mash. Season well with salt and pepper.

A little truffle oil stirred in at the end, or, even better, a truffle shaved over the top is always an added bonus.

Any leftover mash can be baked in the oven, spotted with butter, until crisp on the top.

Braised Courgette Flowers and Mint

For this dish you want the flower as well as the actual courgette. The flowers don't need to be perfect, a bit rough around the edges is fine. I had this cooked for me in Lucca – it came to the table in large bowls, with bread, and that was all. I am always trying to remember that less is more, but those Italians have perfected the simplicity of cooking. In Italy they use a wild mint that can be incorporated at the beginning of the cooking, while our fresh mint is better added at the end. Don't worry if you can't find courgettes with flowers – the dish will still be lovely.

SERVES 4

450g courgettes, with flowers
50ml olive oil
2 cloves of garlic
½ a lemon
a handful of fresh mint, chopped
sea salt and freshly ground black pepper

Slice the courgettes thinly and roughly, or just do them in a food processor using the slicer. Heat the olive oil in a frying pan and add the bashed garlic cloves. Turn the heat down so you don't get any colour on the garlic. Cook until soft, then discard the garlic.

Add the sliced courgettes and keep frying – a little colour on the courgettes is good. As they begin to colour and soften, add the flowers and cook until they start to wilt. Add a squeeze of lemon and a sprinkle of mint and season with salt and pepper.

Good on garlic toast, or with grilled beef.

Braised Chard and Fennel

This dish can be used in many ways – I like to serve it as a vegetable dish in its own right, with a little crumbled goat's cheese on top, but it can also be used as a base for a risotto, and it goes well with meat or fish as a side dish. It's lovely with polenta, too, and can be mixed with eggs to make a great tortilla.

SERVES 4

250g Swiss chard
5 tablespoons olive oil
4 shallots, quartered lengthways
1 large clove of garlic, crushed
1 bulb of fennel, cut into wedges
200ml dry white wine
sea salt and freshly ground black pepper
120g goat's cheese

Rip the chard leaves from their stalks and set aside. Slice the stalks crossways into 2cm lengths, then wash both leaves and stalks, keeping them separate. Heat 3 tablespoons of olive oil in a deep frying pan, add the shallots and half the crushed garlic and cook gently on a medium heat for 5–10 minutes. Add the chard stalks, fennel and wine and cook gently for about 20 minutes, until the stalks and fennel have softened. Season with salt and pepper as you go.

In another pan heat the remaining 2 tablespoons of olive oil. Add the rest of the crushed garlic and cook for 1 minute, then add the chard leaves. Let them cook for 2 minutes, then season with salt and pepper and add them to the fennel mixture. Spoon on to a large serving plate and crumble the goat's cheese on top.

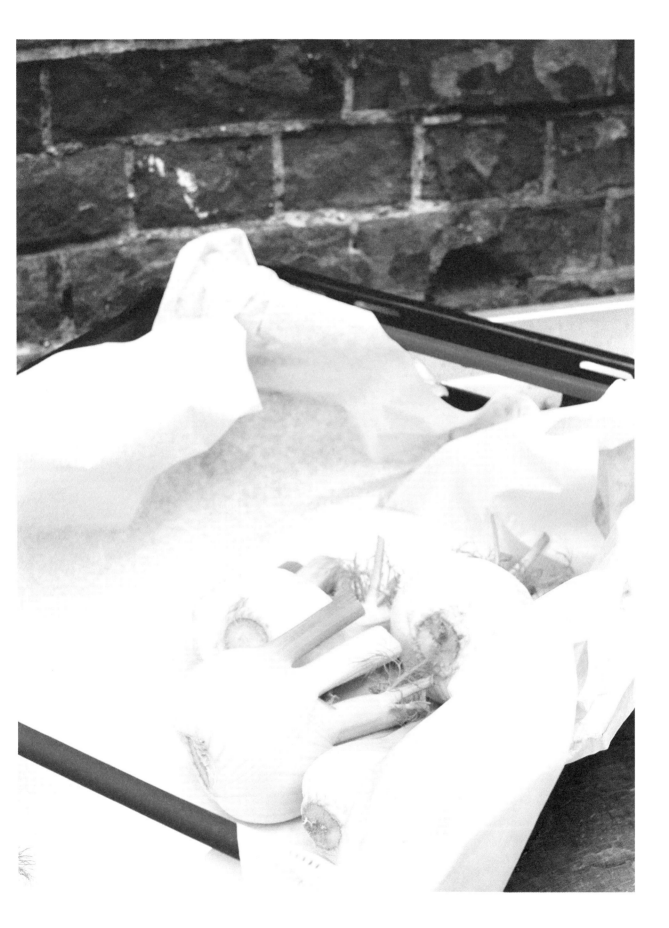

Braised Fennel and Olives

SERVES 6

4 bulbs of fennel
200ml olive oil
5 cloves of garlic
zest of 1 lemon, removed in strips
½ a bottle of dry white wine
sea salt and freshly ground black pepper
a small bunch of fresh thyme
4 bay leaves
a handful of black Kalamata olives

Preheat the oven to 180°C/fan 160°C/350°F/gas 4.

Slice each fennel bulb into 6 wedges. Heat the oil in a deep frying pan and sauté the fennel, stirring occasionally, until lightly browned. Add the whole peeled garlic cloves and the lemon zest and continue to cook for 4 minutes. Add the wine, salt and pepper and bring to the boil for a few minutes. Tie the herbs together and add to the pan, then scatter over the olives.

Transfer everything to a baking dish and season with more salt and pepper. Cover with foil and cook for 45 minutes, until the fennel is tender.

Green Beans and Roast Shallots

It is hard for me to top and tail a green bean without hearing the voice of the great Simon Hopkinson reminding me how important it is to trim both ends.

SERVES 4

6 shallots
olive oil
sea salt and freshly ground black pepper
500g French beans, topped and tailed
vinaigrette (see page 73)
a handful of capers
2 handfuls of watercress, stalks removed

Heat the oven to 180°C/fan 160°C/350°F/gas 4. Put the shallots into a roasting tray with a little olive oil, salt and pepper and cook in the oven for about 20–30 minutes.

Bring a large pan of salted water to the boil. Pop in the beans and cook them for 3 minutes – a little crunch is OK.

Leave to cool, but while they are still warm dress them with vinaigrette, and mix in the chopped roasted shallots, capers and watercress.

Roast Jerusalem Artichokes, Olives and Watercress

Jerusalem artichokes seem to come from a different time, with their knobbly rustic look, and then can turn into such glamour (apart from the farting).

SERVES 4

12 Jerusalem artichokes
5 cloves of garlic, peeled
5 shallots, peeled and cut in half
60ml olive oil
sea salt and freshly ground black pepper
a handful of green olives (Petit Lucques are good, if you can get them)
2 bunches of watercress, picked, washed and spun dry
vinaigrette (see page 73)

Preheat the oven to 180°C/fan 160°C/350°F/gas 4.

Scrub the artichokes well, rinsing away all the dirt from any nook or cranny. Cut in half and pat dry.

In a baking tray mix together the artichokes, garlic and shallots, then coat with the olive oil and season with salt and pepper. Roast in the preheated oven for 40 minutes, until the vegetables are tender (but be careful, don't burn the garlic – turn the temperature down slightly if it's browning too quickly). Add the olives for the final 10 minutes.

Leave to cool, then mix with watercress and a little vinaigrette. A good winter dish.

Angus's Birthday Pickles

This recipe comes from a combination of great cooks: Angus Cook, and Madhur Jaffrey in *An Invitation to Indian Cooking*. Another variation on vegetable pickles, you can eat these on their own before dinner as a snack or to accompany meat dishes. In Japanese culture pickles aid the digestion. So eat loads of them.

During the pickling time the vegetables let off strong odours, so it is best to pickle them outside.

1kg rainbow carrots, peeled and cut into 1cm thick slices
1 beetroot, peeled and cut into quarters
a few fresh chillies
500g small turnips, scrubbed and cut into small wedges
a pinch of saffron
4 litres mineral water
3 teaspoons sea salt
4 tablespoons brown mustard seeds
2 tablespoons coriander seeds

Divide the carrots between 2 metal bowls, and add half the beetroot to one bowl and the chillies to the other.

Place the turnips in another metal bowl. Toast the saffron in a dry pan for a few moments and add to the turnips.

Bring the mineral water to the boil and add the salt. Pour a third of the salty water over each bowl of vegetables. Roughly grind the mustard and coriander seeds and add a tablespoon to each bowl.

Cover each bowl with clingfilm and leave in a place where the smells won't affect you too much. Outside is good. Stir each bowl, with a clean metal spoon, once a day for a week.

Keep the pickles in jars in the fridge if you are not using them straight away. Serve a mixture, in bowls, and enjoy the autumn colours.

PUDDINGS AND CAKES

Often I find that people want to move around after dinner, so little puddings that you can pick up work well – something like chocolate pots or lemon possets, or, if the oranges are around, blood orange possets, are easy to make in quantity. If you are making puddings for large numbers you need to make sure you have enough vessels. Secondhand shops and markets are good places to pick up odd little jars or pots. Small glass jam-jars or yoghurt pots work well. You also need to make sure you have enough fridge space, so clear some shelves so that the puddings can fit in neatly. Make them in the morning, or the day before, so they have enough time to set if they need to.

Making larger quantities is usually quite simple: just double (or treble) the quantities. But be careful with flavours – taste before doubling or trebling things like vanilla pods, as you can easily overdo vanilla and generally will need only one. Spices as well – be careful when doubling these, as you don't want to overdo them.

Puddings that are kept in the freezer also work well for large groups, as they can be made a few days earlier and don't suffer along the way. I love a big central pudding like a tart; all it needs is good cream, so buy the best.

Sweet Shortcrust Pastry

This recipe can be used for all the tart recipes that follow. If you have a large enough freezer you could have some prepared beforehand. Waiting for that moment when you suddenly fancy a tart for pudding.

MAKES 500G PASTRY – *enough for a 26–30cm tart tin*

140g unsalted butter, at room temperature
250g plain flour
100g icing sugar
30g ground almonds
a pinch of salt
1 large egg, lightly beaten

Cut the butter into small pieces and put it into a large mixing bowl. Add the flour, then, using your fingertips, rub the butter and flour together until you have something that looks like fine breadcrumbs.

Add the icing sugar, ground almonds and salt and mix until you have a fine crumble. Then add the egg and bring the dough together with your hands. Pat into a roundish shape, dust with a little flour, then wrap in clingfilm and leave to rest in the fridge for at least half an hour. This relaxes the gluten so that you can roll the pastry more easily and it doesn't shrink in the tin.

Note: This pastry works really well if you make it in a food processor – add all the dry ingredients to the bowl of the processor, then add the cubed butter (which you can use straight from the fridge) and process until it looks like breadcrumbs. Add the egg (you don't need to beat it) and pulse until the mixture clumps together, then remove it from the bowl and press it together. Wrap and chill as above.

To blind bake a tart case

Take the pastry out of the fridge and leave it to soften – 20 minutes if it hasn't been in the fridge very long, an hour if it's been in overnight. Using as little flour as possible, roll it out evenly to a size a little larger than your tart tin, turning the pastry after each roll. Then roll the pastry over the rolling pin and unroll it over the tart tin, leaving a little extra overhanging the edges. Gently press the pastry into the base and sides of the tin and put it into the fridge for 30 minutes to rest.

Preheat the oven to 220°C/fan 200°C/425°F/gas 7. Put a layer of greaseproof paper into the tin and pour in some dried beans or baking beans, enough to cover the base evenly and support the sides so that they don't collapse.

Place the tin on a baking sheet and bake in the preheated oven for 20 minutes.

Remove from the oven and carefully take out the beans. Now you are ready to fill your tart.

Pecan and Chocolate Tart

SERVES 8

500g sweet shortcrust pastry (see page 212)
120g dark chocolate, broken into pieces
50g unsalted butter, cubed
125g pecan nuts
4 large eggs
240ml maple syrup
1 teaspoon vanilla extract

Preheat the oven to 220°C/fan 200°C/425°F/gas 7. Line a deep 26cm tart tin with the pastry and blind bake, following the instructions on page 213. Remove from the oven and set aside to cool. Turn the oven down to 160°C/fan 150°C/ 325°F/gas 3.

Melt the chocolate and butter in a heatproof bowl over a pan of gently simmering water, then set aside and allow to cool to room temperature.

Set aside 24 whole pecan nuts and crumble the rest with your fingers into the base of the cooled cooked pastry case.

Put the eggs, maple syrup and vanilla extract into a large bowl and beat by hand with a large balloon whisk, whisking only to just combine and no more – you don't want it too aerated. Add the melted chocolate and butter and whisk again.

Pour the mixture into the pastry case and arrange the reserved whole nuts on top. Place the tart tin on a baking sheet and bake in the preheated oven for 40 minutes.

Lime and Buttermilk Tart

500g sweet shortcrust pastry (see page 212)
4 large eggs
200g caster sugar
2 tablespoons plain flour
375ml buttermilk
60g butter, melted
1 teaspoon vanilla extract
grated zest of 1 large lime

Preheat the oven to 220°C/fan 200°C/425°F/gas 7. Line a deep 30cm tart tin with the pastry and blind bake, following the instructions on page 213. Remove from the oven and set aside to cool. Turn the oven down to 150°C/fan 140°C/300°F/gas 2.

Put the eggs and sugar into a large bowl and beat together with an electric beater until light and fluffy. Add the flour, buttermilk, melted butter, vanilla extract and lime zest.

Pour the mixture into the pastry case, then place the tart tin on a baking sheet and bake in the preheated oven for about 40–45 minutes.

Pear and Almond Tart

I always find it hard to resist a pear tart. While we were getting this book together, Justine, one of the Canteen's chefs, made this perfect tart, and we all loved it so much we felt it had to be written down.

SERVES 10–12

500g sweet shortcrust pastry (see page 212)
6 poached pears (see page 228)

For the frangipane
250g softened butter
250g caster sugar
5 large eggs
250g ground almonds
50g plain flour

Preheat the oven to 220°C/fan 200°C/425°F/gas 7. Line a deep 30cm tart tin with the pastry and blind bake, following the instructions on page 213. Remove from the oven and set aside to cool. Turn the oven down to 180°C/fan 160°C/350°F/gas 4.

Take the pears out of their liquid and cut them in half. Carefully remove the core, then cut them into 1cm slices.

In a food processor, cream the butter and sugar until light and fluffy, then add the eggs one at a time. Finally add the ground almonds and flour and mix until creamy. Put to one side.

Fill the pastry case with the frangipane mixture and spread out evenly. Arrange the pear slices on the frangipane, fanning them out into a circle.

Place the tart case on a baking sheet and bake in the preheated oven for 40 minutes. It should be light brown and firm to touch. Leave to cool before taking out of the tart case.

Serve with crème fraîche.

Raspberry Shortcake Tart

I was delighted when Justin Gellatly gave me this recipe: it's handy for using up those lovely jars of jam your friends give you over the years.

Justin is one of Britain's most talented bakers and pastry chefs. He always seems to have the right amount of frill and earthiness and never forgets his British roots. He is also probably much to blame for my husband's ever-growing tummy. I had to limit Fergus's sugar intake and ban him from eating more than one pudding a day. Ah well, it's the little things that count.

This shortcake is more successful if eaten soon after baking.

SERVES 8–12

250g unsalted butter, softened
125g caster sugar
125g demerara sugar
zest of 1 lemon
1 vanilla pod, split in half lengthways
2 large egg yolks
500g plain flour
1 teaspoon baking powder
1 x 300g jar of raspberry jam or conserve

Put the butter, both sugars and the lemon zest into the bowl of an electric mixer fitted with a beater attachment and scrape in the seeds from the vanilla pod. Cream together until light and fluffy, then beat in the egg yolks one at a time, followed by the flour and baking powder. Mix together very briefly, just until the mixture starts to come together, then stop the machine and finish mixing by hand (don't over-mix it – you want to keep the pastry short).

Divide the pastry into two pieces: two-thirds for the bottom and one-third for the top. Wrap each piece in baking paper and place the large piece in the fridge and the small piece in the freezer. Leave there for at least 45 minutes.

Take the larger piece of pastry out of the fridge and set aside for 30 minutes to come to room temperature. Lightly flour a work surface, then take your rolling pin and roll the pastry out into a circle roughly 3mm thick. It will be quite crumbly – if it's difficult to roll, put it between two large sheets of clingfilm.

Line a deep 30cm tart case with the pastry, then spoon your raspberry jam on top and spread it out evenly. Take the smaller piece of pastry out of the freezer. Using the large holes of a box grater, grate the pastry evenly over the raspberry jam until the jam is covered. Place in the fridge for 1 hour.

Preheat the oven to 180°C/fan 160°C/350°F/gas 4. Take the tart out of the fridge, put it on a baking sheet, and bake in the preheated oven for about 35–45 minutes, until golden brown. Once baked, place on a rack and let it cool down a little.

Serve warm, with extra thick Jersey cream or vanilla ice cream and some fresh raspberries.

Lemon Tart

500g sweet shortcrust pastry (see page 212)
5 large whole eggs
4 large egg yolks
375g caster sugar
300ml double cream
250ml lemon juice (about 6 large lemons)

Preheat the oven to 220°C/fan 200°C/425°F/gas 7. Line a deep 30cm tart tin with the pastry and blind bake, following the instructions on page 213. Remove from the oven and set aside to cool.

Put the rest of the ingredients into a large bowl and whisk together with a balloon whisk. Set aside to settle, preferably overnight in the fridge.

Preheat the oven again to 130°C/fan 120°C/275°F/gas 1. Pour the mixture into the pastry case, then place the tart tin on a baking sheet and bake in the preheated oven for 1 hour.

Rich Dark Ginger Cake

SERVES 6 FRIENDS AFTER A LONG WALK

125g softened butter
125g dark brown sugar
225g plain flour
2 teaspoons ground ginger
a pinch of salt
2 large eggs
275g black treacle or molasses
50g preserved ginger, sliced, or 100g sultanas
5 tablespoons milk
½ teaspoon bicarbonate of soda

Preheat the oven to 180°C/fan 160°C/350°F/gas 4. Grease a 20cm square loose-bottomed cake tin and line the base with baking parchment.

Put the butter into a mixing bowl and cream well, then add the sugar and continue to beat until light and fluffy. In a separate bowl, sift the flour with the ground ginger and salt. Add the eggs to the creamed mixture one at a time, beating continuously and sprinkling a dessertspoon of the flour into the bowl with each one. Stir in the treacle, the preserved ginger or sultanas, and the remaining flour.

Warm the milk gently in a small pan and add the bicarbonate of soda. Stir at once into the mixture and turn it into the cake tin. Bake in the preheated oven for 50 minutes to 1 hour.

Let the cake cool for 5 minutes in the tin, then take it out and leave it to cool completely on a wire rack.

Steamed Chocolate Cake

Don't cut this before it is cold, like I did in the photograph opposite.

SERVES 16

250g unsalted butter, plus extra for greasing
500g dark chocolate, broken into pieces
10 large eggs, separated
50g caster sugar
35g plain flour

Preheat the oven to 160°C/fan 150°C/325°F/gas 3. Grease the base and sides of a 30cm springform cake tin with butter and line with baking parchment.

Put the chocolate and butter into a medium pan and melt gently together. Mix well, then allow to cool to room temperature.

Put the egg yolks into a bowl with the sugar and beat with an electric beater until the mixture is white and ribbony. Fold in the melted chocolate and butter mixture, then sieve in the flour and fold in. Finally, in a large clean mixing bowl, whisk the egg whites until they form soft peaks. Fold them into the mixture gently but as quickly as you can.

Pour the mixture into the prepared cake tin. Bake in the preheated oven for 20 minutes, then take out of the oven, place a serving plate on top and leave to steam and cool completely, for at least an hour. When cool, you can put it into the fridge, which will give you a firmer cake.

Serve with crème fraîche.

Apple and Plum Crumble

As a kid I always loved making a crumble, getting my hands in there and rubbing that sweet buttery mix together until it was the right consistency. You can express yourself with a crumble by adding oats and nuts. The mixture needs to be buttery and crumbly.

SERVES 6

100g walnuts or almonds
300g plain flour
150g small porridge oats
200g unsalted butter, slightly softened
50g dark brown sugar
100g caster sugar
1 teaspoon ground cinnamon
6 eating apples (e.g. Cox's)
6 ripe plums

Preheat the oven to 200°C/fan 180°C/400°F/gas 6. Put the walnuts or almonds into a small roasting tray and toast in the oven for 5 minutes. Leave to cool, then chop roughly. Reduce the oven temperature to 180°C/fan 160°C/350°F/gas 4.

Put the flour and oats into a large bowl and add the butter, cut into small pieces. Using your fingers, rub the butter into the flour and oats. Once the mixture is crumbly, you can stir in the brown sugar, half the caster sugar, the cinnamon and the chopped nuts.

Peel the apples and cut into 2.5cm chunks. Slice the plums in half and take the stones out, then cut them into quarters. Put the fruit into an ovenproof dish and sprinkle over the remaining caster sugar and 5 tablespoons of cold water.

Cover with the crumble mix but don't press it down too tightly. Bake in the preheated oven for 45–50 minutes – to check whether the fruit is cooked, spear it with a small knife, and if it doesn't slide in easily, cook it for a bit longer (but turn down the oven a bit so that the top doesn't burn). The crumble should be crisp and golden brown.

Serve with custard, cream or vanilla ice cream.

Poached Pears

SERVES 6

200g caster sugar
4 tablespoons Poire William liqueur (optional)
1 vanilla pod, split lengthways
rind of 1 lemon, removed in strips
6 firm Conference pears

Put the sugar into a large pan with 1.5 litres of water and the liqueur, if using. Add the vanilla pod and the lemon rind and bring to the boil, stirring until the sugar has dissolved. Turn down to a gentle simmer.

Peel the pears, keeping them whole, and add them to the pan. Bring back to a simmer, cover the pan tightly, and cook over a low heat for about 15 minutes, until the pears are tender. Test them with a thin knife – it should slide in easily. Remove the pan from the heat and leave the pears to cool in the liquid. Pop into the fridge until needed.

Cut into wedges and mix with poached rhubarb (see page 39). For pudding serve with shortbread and crème fraîche.

Custard

250ml whole milk
250ml double cream
1 vanilla pod, split lengthways
4 large egg yolks
40g caster sugar

Put the milk and cream into a pan with the split vanilla pod. Bring almost to the boil, then take off the heat and set aside.

Put the egg yolks into a bowl with the sugar. Beat together with an electric whisk for about 5 minutes, until the mixture is thick and pale and forms a ribbon pattern when you lift the whisk. Slowly, slowly whisk the hot milk and cream into the egg mixture, beating all the time. Return it to the pan over a very low heat, or even better use a double boiler, and stir gently and continuously with a wooden spoon for a few minutes, until the custard has thickened.

Remove the vanilla pod before serving.

Feijoa Ice Cream

I grew up with feijoas, along with Chinese gooseberries (kiwi fruit) and tamarillos, wonderful exotic fruits. Instantly I have wonderful memories of boxes of apricots, peaches and freshly picked kiwi fruit. All a bit wobbly-shaped and smaller than fruits today, but oozing with flavour. You can buy feijoas in posh food halls, such as Harrods. If you can't get them, figs work well instead.

SERVES 6–8

400g ripe feijoas
juice of 1 lemon
1 tablespoon vodka
1 teaspoon Cointreau
175g caster sugar
250ml double cream
250ml whole milk

Trim the feijoas top and bottom, then halve or quarter them. Put them into a food processor with the lemon juice, vodka, Cointreau and sugar and whiz to a purée. Stir in the cream and milk, then put into an ice cream maker and churn. Once lightly frozen, transfer to a plastic container and put it into the freezer for a further 4 hours at least. It keeps for up to a month.

Remove from the freezer 30 minutes or so before serving, to make scooping easier.

Double Lemon Pudding

A simple soothing pudding, the sort of pudding that will warm any man's heart. Men love creamy warm puddings. Do not fear if the mixture splits as acidity from the lemons will divide the mix. What you have left is three different layers of texture, with a gooey bottom moving to a more spongy top. A good quality pouring cream is a must here.

SERVES 6

200g soft unsalted butter, plus a little for greasing
350g caster sugar
grated zest of 3 lemons
1 teaspoon vanilla essence
8 eggs, separated
100g plain flour, sifted
250ml milk
250ml lemon juice

Preheat the oven to 180°C/fan 160°C/350°F/gas 4.

Cream together the butter, sugar, lemon zest and vanilla in a bowl until white and creamy. Beat in the egg yolks, one at a time. Fold in the flour with a metal spoon, alternating with the milk and lemon juice.

Whisk the egg whites in a large bowl until lightly stiff and fold into the mixture.

Generously grease a 3 litre (22 x 30cm) ovenproof dish and pour in the mixture. Place the dish in a high-sided roasting tin and add boiling water to the tin so that it comes a third of the way up the outside of the dish. Carefully transfer to the middle shelf of the oven and bake for 40 minutes, until golden brown on top and looking set in the middle.

Serve warm, with double cream, or chilled.

Poached Tamarillos

6 tamarillos
200g caster sugar
2 strips of lemon rind
2 splashes of Poire William

Score the tamarillos by making a little cross at one end. Plunge them into boiling water for 10 seconds and leave to cool. When cool enough to handle, peel off the skins.

Put the sugar into a pan with 1.2 litres of water and heat until the sugar has dissolved. Add the tamarillos and the lemon rind and simmer for 10 minutes. Take out the tamarillos, put them into a bowl and set aside, then simmer the liquid until it has reduced. Add the Poire William and pour over the fruit.

Serve with ice cream, custard or yoghurt.

Crème Brûlée

5 large egg yolks
125g caster sugar, plus an extra 6 teaspoons for the top
125ml whole milk
325ml double cream
½ a vanilla pod, split lengthways

Preheat the oven to 150°C/fan 140°C/300°F/gas 2.

Put the egg yolks and sugar into a bowl and beat together with an electric mixer for about 5 minutes, until the mixture is pale and thick, and leaves a ribbon pattern when you lift the beater.

Meanwhile, put the milk and cream into a pan, add the split vanilla pod, and heat gently. Simmer for a few moments, then scrape out the vanilla pod and add the seeds to the mix. (Don't throw out the pod: it can be rinsed, dried and put into a jar with caster sugar, to make vanilla sugar.)

Pour the hot milk and cream on to the egg mixture in a slow stream, whisking continuously. Once amalgamated, pour into 6 individual ramekins or brûlée dishes and place them in a large roasting tray. Pour boiling water into the tray so it comes halfway up the side of the ramekins and bake in the preheated oven for 45 minutes, until just set but still wobbly in the middle.

Remove the ramekins carefully and let them cool to room temperature, then chill in the fridge for at least 4 hours or overnight.

Just before serving, sprinkle each ramekin evenly with a teaspoon of sugar. Use a blowtorch to caramelize the top of each one, and serve.

Turkish Coffee Cake

100g wholemeal flour
100g plain white flour
250g soft brown sugar
2 teaspoons ground cinnamon
½ teaspoon grated nutmeg
½ teaspoon ground coriander
175g butter, cut into cubes
2 teaspoons bicarbonate of soda
250ml soured cream or yoghurt
4 tablespoons freshly brewed espresso coffee
2 eggs, beaten
60g chopped walnuts

Preheat the oven to 180°C/fan 160°C/350°F/gas 4.

Put the flours, sugar and spices into a large bowl and mix together, then rub in the cubed butter until you have an even crumble. Press half the mixture into a deep-sided cake tin measuring about 30 x 18cm.

Stir the bicarbonate of soda into the remaining mixture in the bowl, then add the soured cream, espresso coffee, eggs and chopped nuts. Mix well, then pour into the cake tin and spread evenly with a spatula. Bake in the preheated oven for about 30 minutes, until firm and springy to touch.

Leave to cool completely, then cut into squares or fingers. These will keep in an airtight container for up to 3 days.

Buttermilk Bavarois

SERVES 8

3 leaves of gelatine
400ml double cream
250g caster sugar
½ a vanilla pod, split lengthways
rind of 1 lemon, removed in strips
600ml buttermilk

Put the gelatine leaves into a bowl of cold water and leave to soak for 5 minutes.

Put half the cream into a medium pan and add the caster sugar, split vanilla pod and lemon peel. Bring to a simmer, then remove from the heat. Squeeze the gelatine leaves and add to the warm liquid, stirring to dissolve.

Put the rest of the cream into a bowl and whip until thickened. Add the gelatine mixture, passing it through a sieve and discarding the flavourings. Add the buttermilk and mix well.

Pour either into 8 individual moulds or one larger one. I feel a single pudding can look much more dramatic than several smaller ones. But again, each to their own. Put into the fridge and leave to set for at least 4 hours, or overnight.

When ready to serve, dip the outside of each mould briefly into a shallow bowl of just-boiled water to loosen the edges slightly. Upturn each bavarois on to a plate and serve with poached fruit (see pages 36, 39, 228).

Shortbread

MAKES 40–45

250g softened butter
90g icing sugar, sifted
315g plain flour, sifted
½ a vanilla pod, split lengthways
zest of 1 lemon (optional)
2 tablespoons caster sugar

Using an electric mixer, cream the butter and icing sugar until light and fluffy. Add the flour and scrape in the seeds from the vanilla pod. Add the lemon zest if you fancy it. Bring the dough together with your hands but don't overwork it. Roll it into a log shape and wrap in clingfilm. Refrigerate for at least an hour.

Preheat the oven to 150°C/fan 140°C/300°F/gas 2 and line a large baking tray with non-stick parchment. Remove the dough from the fridge and cut into 5mm rounds. Place them on the baking tray. Bake in the preheated oven for 15 minutes.

Sprinkle the shortbreads with the caster sugar as soon as they come out of the oven and leave them on the tray for 5 minutes. Then transfer to a wire rack to finish cooling. They will keep in an airtight container for about 4 days.

A teaspoon of fennel seeds or finely chopped rosemary leaves can be a cheeky addition. Stir them in with the flour.

Chocolate Pots

These are very light – children love them.

MAKES 10

225g dark chocolate, broken into pieces
375ml double cream
150ml whole milk
3 egg yolks
50g icing sugar

Melt the chocolate in a heatproof bowl over a pan of gently simmering water, then allow to cool to room temperature.

Put the cream and milk into a separate pan and heat until it is just about to boil. Remove from the heat.

Put the egg yolks and icing sugar into a bowl and beat together with an electric mixer for about 5 minutes, until the mixture is voluminous and thick and forms a ribbon pattern when you lift the beater. Very slowly add the hot milk and cream to the egg yolks and sugar, whisking constantly. Whisk in the melted chocolate.

Once everything is mixed together, pour into small individual pots, ramekins or espresso cups and refrigerate for at least 2 hours or overnight before serving.

Serve with a little double cream poured over.

Lemon Possets

Fantastically easy and delicious, these give you that little sugar and lemon hit at the end of a meal, lifting you up for the last part. When blood oranges are in season you can use those instead, if you like, to make blood orange possets.

SERVES 10

8 unwaxed lemons
1.5 litres double cream
500g caster sugar

Remove the rind from 4 of the lemons, using a vegetable peeler. Squeeze the juice from all 8 lemons (you should have around 350ml of juice – rolling the lemons on your work surface before cutting them in half will yield more juice).

Put the cream into a pan with the strips of lemon rind and stir over a low heat until the mixture starts to steam. Add all the sugar and stir until dissolved. Turn the heat off and stir in the lemon juice, then leave to settle for 5 minutes. Strain the mixture through a fine sieve into a large jug, discarding the lemon rind.

Pour into 10 ramekins or small bowls, if you have them, or one medium-sized bowl. Cool to room temperature, then put them into the fridge to set for at least 4 hours or overnight.

Serve with a biscuit such as shortbread (see page 239), and maybe a little cream.

Chocolate Brownies

MAKES ABOUT 24

400g dark chocolate, broken into pieces
300g unsalted butter, diced
5 eggs
500g caster sugar
100g flour
100g hazelnuts

Preheat the oven to 170°C/fan 150°C/325°F/gas 3. Butter a 30cm baking tin and line it with greaseproof paper.

Melt the chocolate and butter in a heatproof bowl over a pan of gently simmering water, then allow to cool to room temperature.

Using an electric beater, beat the eggs and sugar until white and mousse-like. Mix in the melted chocolate and butter. Finally, fold in the flour and hazelnuts.

Bake in the preheated oven for 40–45 minutes – the top should be crisp to the touch. Leave to cool before slicing.

Flapjacks

MAKES 18–24

1kg unsalted butter
500g golden syrup
500g soft brown sugar
1.5kg jumbo oats

Preheat the oven to 180°C/fan 160°C/350°F/gas 4. Melt the butter, syrup and sugar in a large pan, then remove from the heat and add the oats. Mix well and pour into a baking tin measuring about 30 x 20cm. Press firmly down and bake in the preheated oven for 30–35 minutes, until a warm brown colour.

Arnold Circus Biscuits

These are based on an Anzac biscuit from the *Edmonds Cookery Book*, the culinary bible of New Zealand.

MAKES ABOUT 36

100g porridge oats
75g desiccated coconut
100g plain flour
100g caster sugar
50g demerara sugar
100g butter
50g golden syrup
1 teaspoon bicarbonate of soda

Preheat the oven to 180°C/fan 160°C/350°F/gas 4, and line 2 baking trays with baking paper.

Put the oats, coconut, flour and both sugars into a large bowl and mix to combine.

Put the butter into a pan and add the golden syrup. Heat slowly and stir with a wooden spoon until the butter and syrup have melted together. Put the bicarbonate of soda into a cup, add 2 tablespoons of boiling water and mix to dissolve. Pour the mixture into the pan. Stir with a wooden spoon, then tip into the dry ingredients and mix to a crumbly paste.

Take teaspoonfuls of the mixture and roll them into balls. Place them on the cold baking trays, leaving a space of at least 3cm between them because they will spread as they cook. Bake for about 12 minutes, until they have spread out nicely and are a dark golden colour.

Cool on a rack, then store in an airtight tin.

CHEESE

Cheese thoughts

Cheese and red wine at the end of a meal are unbeatable, the best; once you start it's hard to stop. I have always been a cheese person – Mum would have a massive block of mousetrap Cheddar in the fridge and Dad would always have a Camembert. I loved a good strong cheese as a kid, and still do. Being a savoury person, a cheese always beats a pudding for me. The French are cheese geniuses. Let's hope boring hygiene rules will not ruin hundreds of years of cheese culture.

Probably my all-time favourite is **Rocamadour**. Goat at its best, and what a name. I first tasted these little white morsels while staying on a riverbank outside Souillac in the Lot (where they also make Vieille Prune). An impressive town. Every corner of the markets in Souillac and the nearby towns had a cheese maker selling trays of Rocamadour. Young or old, soft or hard, it's still delicious. Good to eat after a long summer lunch, preferably on a riverbank in France.

A main course should always be followed by a green salad and cheese. Sometimes it may feel like a lot to fit in or get down. I would say in that case drop the dessert and have cheese. Serving a great cheese at the end of dinner is a fine way to end. It's better to celebrate one cheese (or perhaps two) rather than put out lots of smaller pieces. If you are having a large party, put a whole cheese down and watch it disappear as it moves around the table.

Berkswell is a beautiful hard cheese made in the Midlands, perfect for a large table. The flavour is gentle and nutty, very moreish, and it has a slightly grainy texture. Best sliced thinly and eaten with an oatcake, or a rye crispbread, it's also a good traveller. If you are heading on holiday you need a cheese that won't collapse by the time you arrive.

These are good times if you are into cheese, as we have the most amazing cheese shops, run by people who are expert in every way in their field. Neal's Yard and La Fromagerie have changed the world of cheese in London and led to great cheese shops opening all over the country, saving the many brilliant cheese makers who are struggling away producing some of the best cheeses you can find anywhere. Cheese making is back and may save the world, where landlords and the City have let us down. I say buy more cheese.

Here are a few of my favourites:

British Cheddars, like **Keen's** and **Montgomery**, are genius; maybe a little large to bring out whole, but a really generous chunk is perfect on the table. These Cheddars can turn a boring cheese and tomato sandwich into something fit for a glamorous party.

Crottin.

It's hard to beat a whole **Brie** or **Berkswell**.

When travelling always take a large piece of **Parmesan**. Parmesan is a god of cheese – again, when it has the right gritty texture you know you have struck gold. Investing in Parmesan is a very wise move.

Spenwood, **Caerphilly**.

Kirkham's Lancashire with an Eccles cake.

I nearly forgot **Wigmore**, creamy and very unctuous. Anne and Andy Wigmore make this wonderful cheese. It's soft but not too soft. Perfect for a snack when you're feeling a little peckish.

I like oatcakes with my cheese. I always keep a few packets in the cupboard, generally nothing too fancy – I don't even really like the too rough oatcakes. Toasted raisin bread is delicious with goat's cheese. Melanie finds a little butter with her cheese and biscuit essential. Good cheese and oatcakes: what more could you want? Maybe a glass of wine?

PARTIES

Serve your guests a drink when they arrive, a cocktail, or champagne. Something that lifts the spirits, leaving the trials of the day behind, is pure fun. A gin and tonic is the perfect cocktail – the smell, the taste, the sound, are all as important as the lift. Americans are great at cocktails. There is the tradition of the cocktail hour, and they know about ice, the shape of a glass, the power of a good bartender. The talk, the charm, it should be pleasure.

At home, if you are without a genius bartender, make a simpler cocktail. Jugs of drinks like Negronis are good; they can be poured over ice and it's nice to wander about topping up glasses. It's an enjoyable hostly job. If you're having a big party, have someone on the door so you're not stuck there all evening. If you have a few teenagers around, they can take it in turns.

Canapés should be interesting and tasty little morsels. They do need to be eaten almost immediately, though some dishes will sit around for longer. It's always tricky to work out how many different canapés to serve – around seven is a good number for a two-hour drinks party. Go for an odd number when it comes to candles, flowers or servings; they work better. If you are trying to fill your guests up, you will need to double that.

They shouldn't be too big either – between two and five bites is good, with no overly sloppy fillings or toppings. Beetroot is always a tricky one. You don't want to stain your lovely carpets, or your guests' lovely clothes. Make sure you have lots of small napkins.

Generally you should just make sure you have a few meat canapés, a few fish ones and a few vegetarian ones, so there's something for everyone. And some bowls of nibbly bits, olives, or really good crisps. If you're short of people to help with passing things round, or in the kitchen to put things together, you could have a big bowl of something like mackerel pâté or rillettes, and a great pile of toast, and let everyone do it for themselves. In the summer, bowls of fresh vegetables are lovely, with vinaigrette or anchovy dressing to dip into. Finish with a little sweet treat, such as chocolate brownies, cut into small squares.

Rather boringly, the more you clear up the less likely you are to have breakages. Some mess is good, though, and people stay longer with some happy chaos around them.

Drinks

Glasses

The first question is, long or short stems? I prefer a short stem: Venetian glass is my favourite but it's pricey. The club goblet has always served us well. A multitasking glass, it can be used for anything from champagne to cocktails and wines. Club goblets are great for parties, as they aren't so easily knocked over, and they're not too expensive, which is handy if there are a lot of breakages – and there are always going to be more breakages when there are no waiters clearing as you go.

Wine cocktails

Bicicletta

A clever and refreshing drink, good outside on a hot day. Use a cheapish Italian white – the Campari helps the wine along. Some Italian bars refuse to serve a bicicletta – they think of it like a snakebite. It's named after Italian gentlemen fond of the tipple who weave their way home on their bicycles afterwards.

Campari
white wine

Pour a splash of Campari into a wine glass containing several lumps of ice and top up with white wine – you want it to be a gentle orange-pink colour.

Kir

crème de cassis
white wine, or champagne for a Kir Royale

Pour a tiny bit of cassis into a wine glass and top up with chilled wine. You really don't want too much cassis – it's not like making squash. Experiment a bit until you get a lovely pale colour and the flavour of the cassis.

Champagne

Always a lovely uplifting moment. The better the champagne the better the lift. Ruinart is one of my favourites – gentle on the bubbles and a great name. People love a saucer glass: I love saucers, as they have a feeling of old glamour, although I advise not too much movement with a saucer as it's always a bit tricky.

Black Velvet

The perfect drink for a birthday breakfast. Best served in a pewter or silver tankard if you have any, otherwise a half-pint glass.

Pour in champagne, about half to three-quarters full, and slowly top up with Guinness. Both can be poured into jugs beforehand and then into the glasses as needed – this will cut down on the froth. It's also important to pour the Guinness last, otherwise you get a massive amount of froth.

Champagne Cocktail

white sugar cubes
Angostura bitters
cognac
champagne

Put a sugar cube in the bottom of each champagne flute, drip a few drops of bitters on to the cube, add a couple of dashes of cognac and top up with chilled champagne.

Bellini

white peach purée, or pear purée
champagne

Pour a couple of centimetres or so of chilled peach or pear purée into the bottom of a champagne glass and top up with chilled champagne. Stir.

Beer and cider

Mulled Cider

1 apple
1 orange
1 lemon
4 cloves
1.2 litres cider
1 wine glass of Calvados

1 teaspoon brown sugar
1 apple teabag
600ml water
1 stick of cinnamon
4 allspice berries
2 bay leaves

Wash all the fruit. Slice and core the apple. With a peeler carefully take the rind off the orange and squeeze the juice. Spike the lemon with the cloves. Put the fruit into a large pan with the rest of the ingredients and slowly bring to a simmer. Simmer for 1 hour – do not let it boil. Taste and add more Calvados if needed. Rum also works well if you don't have calvados.

Serve warm, while watching fireworks.

Ale

A barrel of beer always looks good and seems to go a long way, perhaps because women don't drink so much of it. You will need your barrel to be delivered several hours before you need it and set up so that it will settle and be fit for drinking. Barrels are great for weddings and parties.

Best to go local as much as possible. Say you are in Gloucestershire or near by, a barrel of Uley will be a great addition to your party and will charm all the young men.

Guinness

Looks beautiful, revives everyone and seems to be full of goodness. Great as above (page 259) with champagne, but you can also use it to braise beef with, and it's a key ingredient in Welsh rarebit.

Gin

Gin, gin, beautiful gin. The gorgeous sound of early evening, ice clinking against the glass as it swims in Tanqueray . . . Best drunk before dinner, on any evening, hot or cold. There are lots of delicious gins to choose from, but a good staple is Tanqueray.

Gin and Tonic

When life throws you lemons, cut them up and make gin and tonic.

gin	ice cubes
a good tonic – easy on the tonic	a hunk of lemon or lime

Pour the gin, add tonic and ice, and drop in the lemon or lime.
Serve in an old-fashioned glass.

Gimlet

3 shots of gin	1 shot of Rose's Lime Cordial
ice	a twist of lime peel

Shake the gin and lime with ice and strain into a martini glass. Garnish with a lime twist.

Negroni

6 shots of gin	ice
6 shots of Punt e Mes	orange slices
6 shots of Campari	

For a party make this cocktail in jugs. Mix the gin, Punt e Mes and Campari together with a stirrer and pour over ice into an old-fashioned glass or a club goblet. Garnish with a slice of orange. Wait for a few moments and then listen for the Negroni roar once the room has consumed a jug or two.

Gin Martini or Vodka Martini

In the words of Fergus Henderson, 'I'll have a gin martini, with a twist, painfully cold and painfully dry.' The barmen at Dukes serve a brilliant martini, with a little wiggle of their bottom. Don't forget the rule: never more than two. Otherwise you will be a goner.

As with all drinks, I prefer somebody else to make them for me – they always taste better. A martini is one of those drinks that everyone has their own special way of doing.

It's best to keep all the ingredients in the fridge, so they are good and cold. The glasses should be icy cold from the freezer – it's all about cold and dry and heady deliciousness. Lemon peel or olives is a personal choice.

a bag of ice
3 shots of icy cold Tanqueray gin or Russian Standard vodka
½ a shot of Noilly Prat or other dry vermouth
lemons
olives in brine

1. Dip your martini glasses in water, so they are slightly damp but no more, then put the glasses into the freezer for 1–2 hours before you want to make the martini.
2. In a glass jug or a cocktail shaker, swirl a good amount of ice around until it is good and cold.
3. Pour the gin or vodka over the ice, and stir.
4. Pour the vermouth over the gin or vodka.
5. Discard the ice.
6. Pour the cold gin or vodka into the glass.
7. Twist the lemon peel, brush the edges of the glass and slip the lemon twist into the alcohol. Or add an olive.
8. Serve immediately.

Vodka

Russian Standard vodka: very good taste, very good price. That was the mantra in Moscow when we were out there doing a dinner at the Garage. Also, it has a good bottle and it's always lovely to have pretty bottles on the bar or running down the table when you're having a party or dinner.

Bloody Mary

For the Bloody Mary mix
1 teaspoon freshly grated horseradish
1 teaspoon English mustard
1 teaspoon Dijon mustard
3 drops of Tabasco
1 teaspoon Worcestershire sauce
4 grinds of black pepper

juice of 2 lemons
2 litres tomato juice
a pinch of celery salt

To finish the drink
vodka
ice cubes

Try to make the Bloody Mary mix a week before using. Mix all the ingredients together and decant into 2 bottles. Leave them in the fridge until needed.

To finish off the drink, pour 5 shots of vodka into a 1.2 litre jug and top up with a bottle of the Bloody Mary mix. Stir and taste for seasoning, lemon and, of course, vodka. Pour over half a glass of ice cubes.

Moscow Mule

An uplifting, easy drink, good for late-night parties. West London loves a Moscow Mule.

lots of fresh limes
ice cubes

vodka
ginger beer

You can make this in a jug. Pour the juice of about 10 limes into a large jug, drop in some ice, then add about three-quarters of a bottle of vodka. Top up with a couple of small bottles of good ginger beer. Drop in a few lime chunks as well.

Tequila

Margarita

Cointreau
lime juice
tequila
ice cubes

This is another drink you can make easily in a jug. Proportions are 1:2:3, Cointreau, lime juice, tequila – i.e. one part Cointreau, two parts lime juice, three parts tequila. Stir well, with ice. You can slide lime round the edge of the glass and dip the rim lightly in salt, but not too much. Serve in a cocktail glass or an old-fashioned.

Rum

Is best straight, but how about a …

Dark and Stormy

dark rum (try Zacapa)
fresh lime juice
ice cubes
ginger beer

Pour a few centimetres of rum into a tall glass, add a splash of lime, lots of ice and fill up with a good ginger beer. Very refreshing.

After dinner

Vieille Prune, Poire William and grappa are all helpful in aiding the digestion, but can also be a killer the next day. That's when you need green tea to help you back on the road. Vieille Prune is made from prunes and produced in Souillac. For big parties, magnums of Vieille Prune look wonderful and very glamorous.

Whisky

Lagavulin is my favourite malt. We often serve a malt whisky in small glasses with water on the side, with coffee as a little after-dinner treat.

Coffee and tea

Mint Tea

sprigs of fresh mint
boiling water

Put a handful of mint stalks, leaves and all, into a teapot, the prettiest you can find. Pour on boiling water and leave to infuse. Serve in glasses, with sugar or honey on the side.

Cowboy Coffee

4 tablespoons coffee, strong and filter ground
boiling water

At home we use enamel jugs for this, to make it look more cowboy-like. Make sure you use enough coffee.

Pour the hot water over the coffee and leave to settle for about 5 minutes. Stir in one direction, leave for 4 minutes, then stir again in the same direction. Leave to settle and, voilà, the grains will have dropped to the bottom. Serve in small espresso cups with raw sugar on the side. And small glasses of something strong, like Vieille Prune.

Canapés

Nibbles

We always like to have a few bowls of nibbles when guests arrive. These are more about shopping than cooking: little yummies to keep everyone going until their meal is ready. Large bowls of olives and almonds look dramatic; alternatively, as in Italy, lovely small silver bowls with sticks and napkins have a glamorous look. All these nibbles help the drinks to slip down and keep starvation at bay until the serious food arrives.

Olives

We buy the early harvest Petit Lucques, from the Fresh Olive Company; they do brilliant capers, cornichons and all that kind of stuff, and they come in very useful green buckets that can be found in many fridges in London. I love their tangy youthfulness – perfect for the cocktail hour.

Salami, Crisps and Sausages

When on a rock by the sea, I prefer Kalamata olives, with a slice of salami. We usually buy a whole Napoli salami before going away for a holiday in Britain. I like them softer rather than hard.

We get Portuguese crisps from Leila's Shop on Calvert Avenue. I am constantly banging on about the wonders of her shop: everything is beautiful, delicious and unpretentious. It's a proper shop. The crisps are very thin, very crisp, not too salty and quite straightforward. They also taste of potato.

The Polish sausages she has are perfect to serve for dinners, lunches and picnics. A lovely pile of smoked sausages: everyone can dig in and snap the thin ones, slice the fatter ones and dip them into a beetroot relish or horseradish. They are excellent washed down with a lager – though I'm not really a lager girl, and prefer a glass of wine.

Radishes

A plate of crisp radishes nestles in well around more complex, rich canapés, brightening the table. Dipped into celery salt or alongside cold butter, they are a refreshing way to start your party.

Radishes are a favourite of mine, although they can be a lot of work, as you need to wash them carefully and pick off any dead leaves (it's important to leave the good leaves on, though, as they can also be munched up). I like strong and peppery radishes as well as the more gentle breakfast ones. They are the perfect snack before dinner, as they don't fill you up too much and go very nicely with a gin and tonic.

3 bunches of breakfast radishes
cold unsalted butter
sea salt or celery salt

First – and quickly – get the rubber bands off of the radishes and wash them in a lot of cold water. Revive the wee things. Trim off the ends and pick away any nasty leaves. If the leaves are not up to scratch, take a deep breath and trim them all off. Lay the radishes out on your favourite platter with a pile of salt or celery salt, and get dipping.

Gull's and Quail's Eggs

A bowl of boiled eggs in their shells is always an inviting sight. If you see a cluster of people chatting away as they crack shells and nibble on yolks, you know you're in the right party.

The moment for gull's eggs is very short – from mid April to mid May – but when in season they are a sublime spring treat. The eggs are extracted from the nests of black-headed gulls and the shells are beautiful, the perfect size for eating while standing at a drinks party. Mayonnaise or an anchovy dolloped on top is an added bonus.

Quail's eggs are fun and pretty, with those gorgeous shells that are such a nightmare to peel. Plunge them into cold water with a little vinegar added to it after cooking, and, if you are peeling loads, do it under a running tap. The water gets under the membrane and the shells seem to come away a little more easily.

Cheese Straws

These can be prepared beforehand and kept in the freezer until you want to bake them.

MAKES 50–60

1 x 375g pack of puff pastry
1 egg, beaten
150g Montgomery Cheddar, or other good extra mature Cheddar cheese, finely grated
a few good pinches of ground paprika or togarashi (see page 32)

Preheat the oven to 200°C/fan 180°C/400°F/gas 6.

Take the pastry out of the fridge about 20 minutes before you need it. Roll it out 3–4mm thick, then put it on a baking tray and pop it back into the fridge for 20 minutes – if the pastry is warm it's harder to work with.

Cut it in half, brushing both halves with the beaten egg, and sprinkle with the cheese and either paprika or togarashi. With a sharp knife slice the pastry into strips 1–1.5cm wide and about 12cm long. You should have about 50–60.

Twist the pastry strips from both ends, and lay them out on trays lined with greaseproof paper. Bake in the preheated oven for 15–20 minutes, until golden brown and crisp.

Padrón Peppers

Brindisa supply delicious Padrón peppers, which go very well with a hunk of bread and a slice of Serrano ham. Just shallow fry them in olive oil over a high heat and sprinkle with sea salt before serving.

Serrano Ham

For a nibble at a wedding it is splendid and festive to have a ham on a stand with a carver – it makes for delicious theatre.

I love to watch a ham being worked away at the leg, and the careful removal of that delicious fat to expose some of the finest cured meat in the world. A carver will work around the bones with a boning knife and then, with a thin long knife, slice perfectly neat and flat pieces of meat.

You can spend large amounts of money on a ham, depending on its age and the animal's diet, although it does go a long way. A cured jamón – even a more straightforward leg – is almost never a disappointment. Invest in a stand, and sharp knives, a boning knife and carving knife. I like a short sliver: easy to pick up and pop straight into your mouth. There is an art, and with practice one improves. Make sure you have loads of plasters. You can of course buy it pre-sliced.

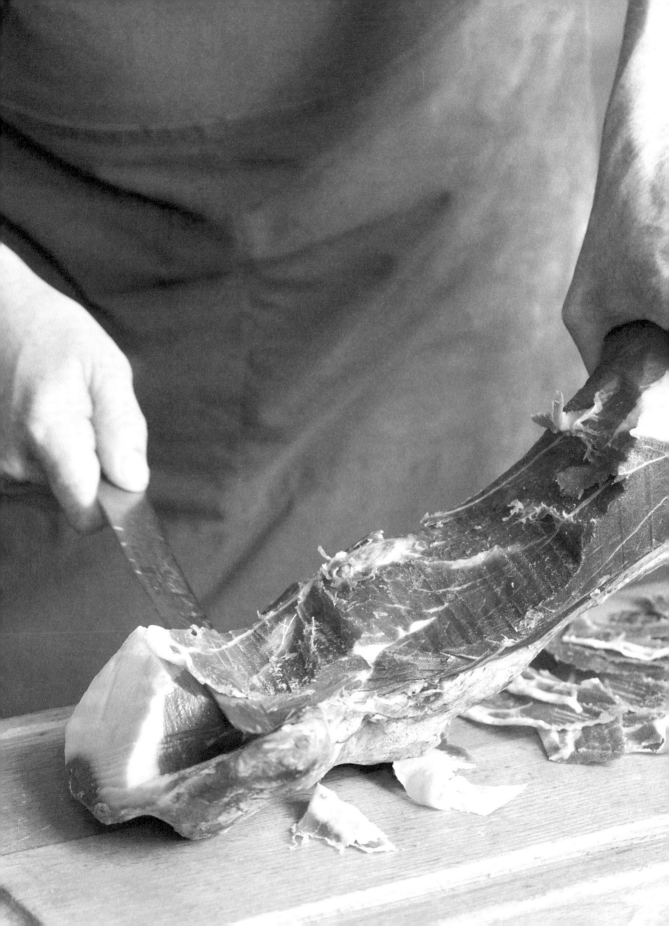

Roast Parsnip Chips

The glamour of the parsnip chip is in the shape – long and crazy.

MAKES ABOUT 32

8 young parsnips
sea salt and freshly ground black pepper
2 tablespoons olive oil
2 tablespoons Dijon mustard
2 cloves of garlic

Preheat the oven to 220°C/fan 200°C/425°F/gas 7.

Peel the parsnips and cut them lengthways into quarters. Blanch in salted boiling water for 4 minutes – this will stop them becoming woody. Drain, then leave them to steam dry in the colander for a couple of minutes.

Put the parsnips on a large baking tray and coat them with the olive oil and mustard. Season with salt and pepper and add the crushed garlic. Mix well, then spread them out in one layer across the tray.

Bake in the preheated oven, turning occasionally, for 20–25 minutes, until cooked through and golden. Then pile on to a platter and serve.

Tomato Toast and Cavolo Nero Pesto

Delicious: toast rubbed with garlic, a little extra virgin olive oil soaked in, then chopped roasted tomatoes. The cavolo nero pesto works really well with it, as does the more traditional basil pesto.

SERVES 6–8

4 plum tomatoes
sea salt and freshly ground black pepper
6–8 slices of sourdough bread
a little extra virgin olive oil
1 clove of garlic, cut in half

For the cavolo nero pesto
400g cavolo nero
100g pine nuts
2 cloves of garlic
100g Berkswell cheese
150ml olive oil

Preheat the oven to 180°C/fan 160°C/350°F/gas 4.

Cut the tomatoes in half, season with salt and pepper, and place on a baking tray. Roast in the preheated oven for 40 minutes: it's best if they get some colour. Leave to one side to cool down.

When cool enough to handle, chop the tomatoes up into a rough mush, stir in the juices from the tray, and check for seasoning.

To make the pesto, rip the leaves off the cavolo nero, discarding the stalks. Bring a pan of salted water to the boil and blanch the leaves briefly. Refresh in cold water and squeeze out any extra liquid. Toast the pine nuts, then put everything into a food processor and blend together lightly. Season with salt and pepper.

Toast the bread and rub it with a little olive oil and the cut side of the garlic. Cut it into 2cm wide fingers and serve the tomatoes on top, with the cavolo nero pesto spooned over.

Red Pepper Toasts

2 red peppers
2 tablespoons extra virgin olive oil
1 teaspoon balsamic vinegar
sea salt and freshly ground black pepper
1 teaspoon capers
8 slices of sourdough bread
100g goat's curd or soft goat's cheese

Preheat the oven to 200°C/fan 180°C/400°F/gas 6.

Rub the peppers with a little olive oil, put into a baking tray and roast whole for about 30 minutes, turning once, until they are blackened all over. Put them into a bowl and cover with clingfilm – this will allow them to steam a bit and help you to peel the skins off more easily. When they are cool enough to handle, remove the skins, cut each pepper in half and take out all the seeds.

Slice the peppers into long thin strips and put them into a bowl. Add the olive oil and balsamic vinegar, and season with salt and pepper. Capers also make a good addition.

Toast the bread either in the oven or on a wood-burning barbecue. Spread with a little goat's curd or cheese, then plop a little of the peppers on top. Serve in rows, like little soldiers.

Tapenade on Toast

I hadn't made a tapenade in years – I was even a little snooty about it as a canapé. Then I discovered the Kalamata olives in Leila's Shop: big fat juicy black olives. The young man who sells them to Leila gets them from his father and they are marinated in their olive oil. They're strong and hearty in flavour and perfect for tapenade. You need a good olive. The other rule with olives is to never buy an olive without a stone.

It's very handy to have in the fridge: perfect on toast as canapés, but also good in pastas, on the side of grilled meats, or fish, in sandwiches. And it's much, much better if you make your own.

SERVES 6–8

200g Kalamata olives
2 cloves of garlic
2 tablespoons fresh flat-leaf parsley leaves
2 tablespoons oregano, fresh or dried
4 anchovies
2 tablespoons capers
1 lemon
50ml extra virgin olive oil
sea salt and freshly ground black pepper
6–8 slices of sourdough bread

Stone and chop the olives. Chop the garlic and herbs. Chop the anchovies. Put the olives, garlic, herbs and anchovies into a bowl, add the capers, squeeze in some lemon juice and finish with the olive oil.

Mix everything together, season with salt and pepper, then taste and season again. The texture should be fine but not too fine. It is good to have some texture and not just a paste.

Toast the bread in a toaster, or under a grill, or on a barbecue. Cut into 2cm wide pieces and spread with the tapenade.

Anchovy Toast

6 cloves of garlic, unpeeled
100ml extra virgin olive oil, plus a little for roasting
1 tin or jar of anchovies in olive oil
1 tablespoon red wine vinegar
freshly ground black pepper
4–6 slices of sourdough bread

Preheat the oven to 180°C/fan 160°C/350°F/gas 4.

Rub the garlic cloves with a little olive oil and roast for about 25–30 minutes, until the insides are squidgy and can easily be squished out of their skins. Squish all the garlic out of the cloves.

Put the anchovies, roasted garlic and vinegar into a food processor and whiz together, then very slowly add the olive oil. Grind in a few rounds of pepper. Taste. It should be a smooth, thick paste.

Toast the bread in a toaster, or under a grill, or on a barbecue. Cut into 2cm wide pieces and spread them thickly with the anchovy gunge.

Sea Bass Ceviche

This makes a lovely canapé. It can be served either in little gem leaves or on Italian crisp bread – both are good vehicles for this topping. It is a very elegant and refreshing dish. I always use the stalks of coriander – saves all that picking, and if you chop them finely the stalks are as tasty as the leaves.

MAKES 10

1 cucumber
1 fresh red chilli
2 shallots
100ml extra virgin olive oil
juice of 2 limes
zest of 1 lime
sea salt and freshly ground black pepper
1kg very fresh sea bass fillet, boned and skinned
1 tablespoon very finely chopped fresh coriander

To serve
2 little gems
flat crisp bread

Cut the cucumber in half lengthways and remove the seeds with a teaspoon. Deseed the chilli. Finely dice the cucumber, chilli and shallots and put into a bowl. Add the olive oil, lime juice and zest, and season with salt and pepper.

Using a sharp knife, thinly slice the sea bass – it should be wafer thin. Spread the slices out beautifully on a platter, pretending you are a sushi chef – each slice should be meant. Add the coriander to the dressing and pour over the fish. The ceviche can be served immediately.

Wash and dry the little gem leaves – you need 10 of them. Serve a little of the ceviche and dressing inside the leaves. Alternatively, break the crisp bread into small pieces and top each one with a teaspoon of ceviche.

Feta and Parsley Parcels

These little parcels can be made before a party and they freeze very well.

MAKES ABOUT 20 CANAPÉ-SIZE PARCELS

a bunch of fresh flat-leaf parsley
150g feta cheese
freshly ground black pepper
1 packet of filo pastry
250g unsalted butter

Pick the leaves off the parsley stalks and chop them to a medium texture.
Put them into a bowl and crumble in the feta – there should be roughly equal
amounts of parsley and feta. Season with pepper.

Take the filo out of the fridge and remove it from the packaging. Roll it in
a slightly damp tea towel – this will stop the pastry drying out. Melt the butter
in a small pan over a low heat.

Carefully lay out a sheet of pastry and use a pastry brush to apply a thin coat
of melted butter. Slice into 5 strips lengthways with a sharp knife. Take a small
teaspoon of the parsley mixture and put it near one end of a pastry strip. Fold
one corner of the pastry over the filling to make a triangle, then fold over and
over again, keeping the triangle shape, until you get to the other end of the strip.
Tuck in the loose end neatly. Repeat with the rest of the pastry and filling.

Preheat the oven to 200°C/ fan 180°C/400°F/gas 6. Brush the parcels with
more butter and place them on a baking tray. Cook in the preheated oven for
10 minutes, until brown and crisp. Eat them as soon as you can pick them up.

Boiled Egg, Little Gem and Anchovy

It is important to make your own mayonnaise for this. Don't boil the eggs for too long – they're better with a bit of yolk ooze. Three of these each also make a good starter.

MAKES 12

2 little gem lettuces
6 eggs
4 tablespoons mayonnaise (see page 172)
12 anchovy fillets in olive oil, drained

First, wash, drain and dry the little gems and pick out the best leaves – you need 12. Make sure you don't rip the leaves: little gems are the best to use here, as they have good structure.

Boil the eggs for just 7 minutes, then leave them under a cold running tap until cool. Just before serving, shell the eggs and cut them in half. Pop each egg half into one of the little gem leaves and blob on a little mayonnaise with a teaspoon. Cut the anchovy fillets at a jaunty angle and place on top.

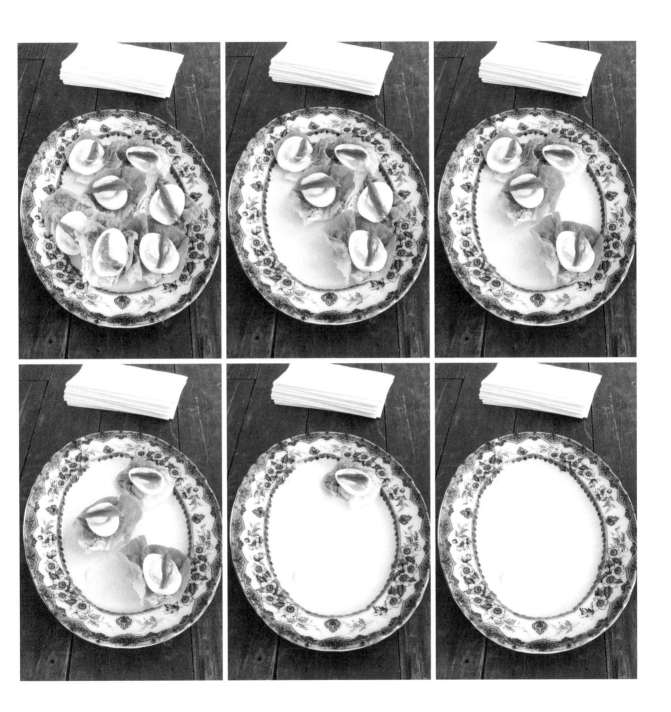

Crab, Chilli and Coriander

MAKES 12

For the crab
1 onion
1 stick of celery
1 bulb of fennel
1 lemon
1 lime
a small bunch of fresh herbs,
  e.g. thyme, bay leaves
2 tablespoons sea salt
1 large live cock crab, weighing about
  1.5kg, or 2 smaller ones (though a
  larger one will be less fiddly to pick)

For the devilled bit
2 spring onions, trimmed
50g fresh ginger
1 teaspoon finely chopped
  fresh red chilli
2 limes
4 heaped tablespoons mayonnaise
  (see page 172)
a bunch of fresh coriander,
  leaves picked and chopped
sea salt and freshly ground black pepper

To serve
12 little gem lettuce leaves
  or 4 pieces of toast

To cook the crab, bring a very large pan of water to the boil. Roughly chop the onion, celery and fennel, and halve the lemon and lime. Add to the pan with the herbs and salt and turn down the heat slightly so that the boil is not too violent. Add the crab and boil gently for 12–15 minutes, depending on its size. Leave to cool in the water.

When the crab has cooled down, twist off the legs and the claws. Push the body section out, using your thumbs, and remove the dead men's fingers – these are the soft brown flaps on either side. Scoop the brown meat out of the large shell with a teaspoon. Remove the flap of shell from the body and cut the body in half. Remove the white meat as best you can, using picks, crackers and cleavers – the more the better. Put the brown and white crabmeat into a bowl.

Cut the spring onions in half down the middle and slice thinly at an angle. Peel and finely grate the ginger, collecting the juice. Add the spring onions, grated ginger, ginger juice and chopped chilli to the crabmeat and mix together, adding lime juice to taste and enough mayonnaise to bring the mixture together. Lastly add the chopped coriander and season with salt and pepper.

Serve in little gem lettuce leaves or on toast fingers. Also good as a starter – three leaves per person.

Devils on Horseback

Pickle the prunes the week before you need them, and have your butcher slice the streaky bacon from its best and happiest side: it's easier if the slices are long and thin.

MAKES 24

24 Agen prunes
12 rashers of streaky bacon
24 cocktail sticks

For the pickling liquid
250g caster sugar
200ml white wine vinegar
200ml water
2 cloves
1 teaspoon coriander seeds
1 stick of cinnamon
½ teaspoon allspice berries
2 strips of lemon rind

To make the pickling liquid, put all the ingredients into a pan, bring to the boil, then reduce the heat and simmer for 20 minutes so that the flavours infuse. Leave to cool, then add the prunes and leave to pickle for 4 days or more.

When you are ready to cook, preheat the oven to 180°C/fan 160°C/350°F/gas 4.

Take the prunes out of the pickling liquid and remove the stones. Lay the bacon on a board, place a sheet of clingfilm on top, and run the rolling pin over it to flatten the rashers slightly. Remove the clingfilm and cut each rasher in half. Neatly wrap a piece of bacon around each prune and keep it in place with a cocktail stick. Place on a baking tray.

Bake in the preheated oven for about 15 minutes, turning them halfway through. When they come out of the oven they can be blistering hot and can burn mouths, so let them cool down a bit and replace the cocktail sticks with fresh ones before serving.

PICNICS AND BARBECUES

Most years we head to a small Scottish island for a summer break. Our days are spent avoiding the rain, cooking hearty meals indoors, playing hours of cards as we wait for our next meal. Or, on one of those rare moments when the sun does come out, we pack massive picnics and head to the beach.

I love to spend a day collecting driftwood and building fires, fighting with the blokes over how or where the fire should be and who is going to cook. It is always a struggle to take control of the barbecue. Men seem to feel it is their rightful place, next to the burning coals, turning the meat, but women also like cooking and carving a piece of meat outside.

Picnic planning and packing is essential, covering all the necessary needs. We generally travel to picnics laden with baskets and ice bins. When I was a kid in New Zealand we would travel to our favourite picnic spots, with Dad carrying a backpack. He always managed to fit in a billy and a few sandwiches, but nothing compared to what I have become accustomed to here.

A simple picnic outing could involve a couple of families, carrying beers, red wine, white wine, corkscrews, and all the food, across a long white beach. Whole legs of lamb, polenta, buns, lemons, olive oil. Lemons and olive oil and salt and pepper can fix anything. Never go without tongs, corkscrews, matches and blankets. It's important to forget a few things though – the stress of it gives everybody something to fight about.

Tupperware is useful – I am obsessed with plastic, the right size of container, with a lid, a perfectly fitting lid. Fill the Tupperware with marinating meats, fish, sauces, salads, breads, and don't forget the cheese (Berkswell is a good traveller), oatcakes and, most important, the fruit-and-nut chocolate, useful for bribing children and teenagers into carrying baskets, blankets and empties back down the beach.

Eating on a windswept rock with the rain threatening has the added bonus of somehow making everything taste better. Cheese and oatcakes can become the most moreish delicious morsel. The struggle makes it all the more pleasurable.

Bun Feast

cured salmon, cucumber and dill
crab mayonnaise
roast sirloin and horseradish
pork belly and apple sauce
Montgomery Cheddar and chutney
chard and Berkswell

Smallish soft buns (see page 19) filled with deliciousness. The bun is a holding vehicle for the perfectly made filling. A big bowl of buns is great for a relaxed social. The above are a few of our favourite fillings, all crowd-pleasers, simple and yummy. They are best made not too far ahead of time, and are lovely to make as your hungry guests hover around.

Slice the buns but leave a hinge. Carefully spread with unsalted butter, making sure each bun has a smooth coating. Add chutneys or sauces: this is the grouting.

Make sure you use thin slices of salmon cut to the right size. The sirloin should be pink and thin – you don't want to be struggling with bits of fat with a glass in your hand. With greens it is better to use the leaf than the stalk.

Cornish Pasties

MAKES 12

For the pastry
1kg self-raising flour
20g cold butter, grated
20g sea salt
250g suet
150ml cold water
plain flour, for dusting
50ml milk
1 egg, beaten, to glaze

For the filling
400g swede
400g waxy potatoes
2 onions
400g skirt steak
2 tablespoons plain flour
1 teaspoon sea salt
1 teaspoon freshly ground black pepper
120g butter

Put the flour and butter into a bowl and rub together. Add the salt, mix in the suet, then add the cold water and bring together with your hands. Form into a ball and leave to rest in the fridge for at least an hour.

To make the filling, peel the swede and potatoes and cut into slices 2cm wide and 0.5cm thick. Slice the onions into thin half-moons. Trim any sinews off the steak. Cut into small pieces similar to the vegetables. Put the prepared beef and vegetables into a bowl and mix in the flour, salt and pepper.

Preheat the oven to 200°C/fan 180°C/400°F/gas 6 and lightly oil 2 large baking trays. Divide the pastry into 4 equal pieces. Lightly flour a work surface and roll out one piece of pastry to about 0.5cm thick. Cut out 3 rounds 18–20cm in diameter, about the size of a bread plate, re-rolling if necessary.

Take one of the pastry rounds and brush all around the edge with milk. Rest half the pastry round on a rolling pin. On the other half, leaving a border, place about 1 tablespoon of the meat filling and add a little knob of butter. Be careful not to use too much filling, otherwise the pasties can burst. Fold over the pastry, to enclose the filling. Using your forefinger and thumb, turn the edge over to form a curl and repeat all round so that the filling is sealed in.

Make 2 more pasties with the remaining pastry rounds, then make 3 more from each piece of pastry – 12 in all. Place them all on the baking trays. Glaze with beaten egg. Cook in the preheated oven for 20 minutes, then turn down the oven to 160°C/fan 150°C/325°F/gas 3 and bake for a further 45 minutes. If the pasties are browning too fast, cover them with greaseproof paper.

Bacon and Egg Pie

This is an old school pie from New Zealand: you are not a proper mother if you don't pack your kids off with a bacon and egg pie for their sports day.

I found it was also very successful on a cold sandy bank in Scotland after the children had spent a night camping. I think their camping involved running around all night and not sleeping, starving because they had eaten all their sausages very early on, so I was 'top mum' arriving with a warm bacon and egg pie.

It feels as if it won't work, but it does and very easily. Peas can be added – always good to get a bit of green in.

SERVES 9–12

250g streaky bacon
30g butter, plus extra for greasing
flour, for dusting
375g frozen puff pastry

2 tomatoes
9 eggs
2 egg yolks
sea salt and freshly ground black pepper

Preheat the oven to 200°C/fan 180°C/400°F/gas 6.

Put the strips of bacon on a baking tray with a few knobs of butter and cook in the preheated oven for 5 minutes or so. Take the bacon out but leave the oven on.

Using a little more butter, grease a rectangular baking tray about 30cm long.

Flour your work surface and roll out the pastry. Cut it in half, then, using a rolling pin, roll out one half until it is large enough to line the baking tray and let the pastry come halfway up the sides of the tray – this is important to prevent the egg leaking out later.

Cover the pastry with the bacon – you may need to break it into strips to make sure that the pastry is evenly covered. Slice the tomatoes and lay them over the bacon. Crack the eggs evenly on top.

Roll out the rest of the pastry, and cut it into thin strips, placing it over the eggs in a lattice pattern.

Beat the egg yolks with a little salt and pepper and glaze the pastry with the mixture, using a pastry brush or your fingers.

Bake in the oven for 30 minutes, until the pastry is golden. Set aside to cool slightly, then cut into pieces and serve with Steinlager.

Scotch Eggs

Everyone loves a Scotch egg – well, maybe not vegetarians. The important thing is to keep checking the seasoning. If you don't have a mincer, ask your butcher to mince the meat for you.

MAKES 15 HEN'S EGG SIZE/36 QUAIL'S EGG CANAPÉ SIZE

500g pork shoulder, minced
500g boneless rindless
    pork belly, minced
200g lardo (cured white
    pork fat), chopped finely
2 red onions
2 teaspoons chopped fresh sage leaves
2 teaspoons fresh thyme leaves
3 cloves of garlic
100g butter

125ml red wine
sea salt and freshly ground black pepper
15 small or medium hen's eggs,
    or 36 quail's eggs
200g plain flour
3 eggs, beaten
150g white panko breadcrumbs
    (from Asian shops)
1.5 litres sunflower oil

Mix together the pork shoulder, belly, and lardo. Finely dice the onion, and mince the sage, thyme and garlic together.

Melt the butter in a pan and add the onions, sage, thyme and garlic. Cook gently for a few minutes, then add the wine and let it bubble away until it has almost disappeared. Leave to cool completely.

Put the minced meats into a large bowl with the onion mixture and mix together. Season well, maybe a little more than usual. (To check the seasoning, cook a little of the mixture in a pan and taste it.)

Boil hen's eggs for 7 minutes and quail's eggs for 2 minutes, and leave them to cool under running cold water. Shell them carefully.

Take approximately 100g of the meat mixture and flatten it out to a round shape under a sheet of clingfilm. Fold it tightly round one of the eggs, making sure there are no holes. Repeat, using the rest of the meat mixture and eggs – you should be able to make 15 Scotch eggs with hen's eggs and 36 with quail's eggs using the amounts given in this recipe.

Line up 3 shallow bowls and place the flour in one bowl, the beaten eggs in another and the panko crumbs in another. Dip each meat-coated egg into flour, shaking off the excess, then dip into beaten egg and finally into the breadcrumbs, coating evenly.

Heat the oil to 160°C in a deep-fat fryer or a large heavy-bottomed pan and fry the eggs in batches, making sure the oil comes back up to temperature before putting in the next lot. Fry hen's eggs for approximately 8 minutes and quail's eggs for 6 minutes, until they are brown, crisp and the meat is cooked.

Carefully remove the eggs from the hot oil with a slotted spoon and drain on kitchen paper. When they have cooled down, serve them whole, halved or quartered.

Long Sandwich

This sandwich oozes glamour, especially if you buy fabulous bread, and make your own chutney and mayonnaise. The onglet, which is the French name for beef skirt, is best cooked over a barbecue, on a beach in Scotland ... but if this isn't possible, a pan and a hot oven work well. This is a good moment for using up any chutneys or odd bods that are wafting around in the fridge. There aren't any rules here, so just express yourself.

SERVES 4

250g onglet
200ml red wine
50ml olive oil, plus extra for roasting
½ a fresh chilli, deseeded and chopped
a few sprigs of fresh thyme and sage
2 bay leaves
2 red onions
sea salt and freshly ground black pepper
4 tomatoes

1 teaspoon balsamic vinegar
a few gherkins, sliced
2 little gem lettuces
a long loaf of bread, or a baguette
butter, for spreading
Dijon mustard, for spreading
chutney, for spreading
mayonnaise (see page 172)

The night before, trim the onglet of any fat and put it into a dish with the red wine, olive oil, chilli and the herbs, tied into a bundle. Leave to marinate overnight.

Preheat the oven to 180°C/fan 160°C/350°F/gas 4. Peel the red onions and cut them into thin wedges. Put them into a roasting tray and toss them with olive oil, salt and pepper. Roast them in the preheated oven, covered with foil, for 20 minutes, then take off the foil and cook for a further 10 minutes.

Meanwhile, cut the tomatoes in half, brush them with olive oil, sprinkle with balsamic vinegar and season with salt and pepper. Put them into a roasting tray and cook them alongside the onions for 15 minutes. When the onions and tomatoes are both ready, remove them from the oven and set aside.

Turn the oven up to 200°C/fan 180°C/400°F/gas 6. Remove the onglet from its marinade and season all over with salt and pepper. Put an ovenproof pan on a high heat and brush with a little oil. When the pan is good and hot, brown the meat all over, then pop it into the oven and cook for 8 minutes. Remove from the oven and let the meat rest for 10 minutes at least. It needs to be rare.

When you're ready to build your sandwich, slice the gherkins. Wash the lettuces and take them apart – the large outer leaves are better for this. Cut the bread in half lengthways, leaving one edge still attached. Then start to build. Spread the bread with butter, then spread Dijon on one half, chutney and mayonnaise on the other. Lay the lettuce leaves on top, then the gherkins, roasted red onions and tomatoes.

Finally, slice the onglet against the grain into thinnish slices and lay them along the sandwich – you may have to push it in a little to fit, don't be timid. Close it up.

On a board, using a good bread knife, slice the sandwich into everyone's preferred width and make sure you have a lot of napkins, as it is a messy business. Perfect with lots of cold Brouilly.

Barbecued Leg of Lamb

1 leg of lamb, boned and butterflied
  (ask your butcher, or see below)
3 tablespoons sea salt
freshly ground black pepper

For the marinade
2 tablespoons olive oil
2 tablespoons sumac (optional)
½ a bottle of white wine
125ml red wine
2 sprigs of fresh rosemary
2 sprigs of fresh thyme
zest of 3 lemons
juice of 1 lemon
6 cloves of garlic, crushed

For the green sauce
2 handfuls of rocket
a handful of fresh mint
a handful of fresh flat-leaf parsley
a small handful of fresh tarragon
a small handful of fresh chervil
a small handful of fresh sorrel
4 cloves of garlic
2 tablespoons capers
1 teaspoon Dijon mustard
1 tablespoon crème fraîche
140ml olive oil
sea salt and freshly ground black pepper

Boning and butterflying the lamb
To bone and butterfly a leg of lamb you need a sharp boning knife. First, to bone the lamb, put it skin side down on a board and slice along the bone on the top of the leg. Follow along the bone, keeping the knife close to it. When the bone loosens, bring the knife around the socket. Sever the tendons, then cut through the joint to remove it. Then move on to the top of the thigh bone, slowly following the bone as closely as possible. Remove the bone once you have cut all around it. Remove the shank bone by cutting along one side of it, then up and around the knee joint and kneecap. Twist the shank and disconnect.

To butterfly the boned leg, cut horizontally into the thickest parts on either side of where the thigh bone was removed and open the lamb outwards. Trim away any extra fat.

The lamb can be grilled whole or in sections. It is easy to follow the sections by sliding a sharp knife along the sinews and just pulling them away. This can be helpful as you will have smaller pieces to handle, and they do cook at different times.

Day 1

When you have boned and butterflied your lamb, put the olive oil, sumac (if using), wine, rosemary, thyme, lemon zest and juice into a large container and mix together well. On a board, open up the butterflied leg of lamb and rub it all over with the crushed garlic. Put the lamb into the marinade, submerging it fully. Cover and leave in the fridge overnight.

Day 2

Take the meat out of the fridge at least an hour before you want to cook it and season it with salt and pepper. The meat needs to be at room temperature.

To make the green sauce, pick the leaves of the rocket and all the herbs off their stalks and chop them reasonably finely. You can use a food processor, but I prefer to chop the herbs by hand individually – you get more texture that way. Put them all into a bowl. Peel and chop the garlic, and if you are using large capers chop them too. Add these to the bowl. Mix the mustard and crème fraîche together and add the olive oil. Add to the bowl of herbs, season with salt and pepper and mix well. Keep the sauce in the fridge until you need it.

Now it's time to start the barbecue, and you need at least an hour for a charcoal fire to burn down. I prefer wood, but this will burn even faster, so don't let the fire burn down too much. You need enough heat to cook your leg of lamb.

Pop the lamb on to the barbecue and cook it for 20 minutes on each side, seasoning it with salt and pepper as it cooks. Keep prodding, turning and moving the pieces around the rack, and try not to burn it. Don't walk off and leave the meat to cook itself. If you have cut it into sections, some may be cooked earlier than others; check by sliding a thin sharp knife into the centre – when it is quite warm to the lip, you are ready to go. Leave the lamb to rest for 10 minutes, wrapped in foil.

Carve the meat into thin slices. Some pieces will be more well done than others, catering for all tastes. If you haven't any plates and you are on a sandy beach or a crazy rock, serve the lamb in buns (see page 19), with little gem leaves and a blob of the green sauce. Toast the buns on the barbecue while the meat is resting.

LIST OF MENUS

Here are some menus, including recipes from this book, from past Arnold &
Henderson events – some useful suggestions for how to plan a meal, even if
you're not entertaining ninety people in summer drizzle.

16TH BIRTHDAY
October / 50 guests

———

Langoustines & Mayonnaise
•
Fattoush with Chicken Wings
•
Chocolate Brownies

80TH BIRTHDAY –
SUNDAY LUNCH
September / 80 guests

———

Radishes & Celery Salt
Fish Soup & Rouille
•
Roast Sirloin & Horseradish
Braised Chard & Fennel
Celeriac Mash
•
Apple & Plum Crumble
Custard

CHRISTMAS PARTY
December / 50 guests

———

(Canapés)
Olives
Cheese Straws
Quail's Eggs & Celery Salt
Parsley & Feta Parcels
Anchovy Toast
•
(Little bowls)
Squid & Potato Stew
Braised Fennel Sausages & Soft Polenta
Pumpkin & Lentil Stew
•
Berkswell & Oatcakes
•
Buttermilk Bavarois
Chocolate Pots

DINNER
February / 230 guests

————

Rabbit Rillettes & Cornichons
Sprouting Broccoli & Anchovy
Vinaigrette
•
Veal Shin & Fennel
Celeriac Mash
•
Double Lemon Pudding
•
Coffee
Mint Tea
Poire William

DINNER FOR A GALLERY OPENING
June / 80 guests

————

Peas in Their Pods
Artichoke Vinaigrette
•
Roast Quails
Lentils, Roast Pumpkin & Watercress
Braised Fennel & Olives
•
Crottin
•
Lemon Posset
Shortbread

DINNER FOR A GALLERY OPENING
January / 240 guests

————

Beetroot Soup
•
Venison Stew
Polenta
Aubergine & Olive Stew
•
Wigmore & Oatcakes
•
Chocolate Cake & Crème Fraîche

DINNER FOR A GALLERY OPENING (VEGETARIAN)
October / 200 guests

————

(Canapés)
Artichoke Heart & Berkswell on Toast
Tomato Toast
Braised Chard on Toast
•
Braised Artichokes, Mint & Rocket
Potato, Cep & Onion Bake
Roast Jerusalem Artichoke,
Olives & Watercress
•
Lemon Tart & Crème Fraîche

BARBECUE IN THE RAIN
July / 90 guests

————

(Canapés)
*Crab, Chilli and Coriander
in Little Gem Leaves
Avocado on Toast
Cod's Roe on Toast
Parsley & Feta Parcels*

•

(On the table)
*Olives
Labneh
Bowl of Raw Vegetables: cucumbers,
tomatoes, peas in pods, broad beans,
chicory, peppers, mint
Fattoush
Flat Breads*

•

*Grilled Leg of Lamb
Merguez
Quails
Sardines*

•

Lime & Buttermilk Tart & Cream

BUFFET MENU
October / 80 guests

————

*Olives
Almonds*

•

*Confit Duck, Lentil
& Pickled Vegetable Salad
Roast Roots
Green Beans & Roast Shallots*

•

*Mixed Berry Compote
& Jersey Cream*

WINTER WEDDING
December / 150 guests

————

(Canapés)
*Parsnip Crisps
Scotch Eggs
Fried Whitebait & Tartare Sauce
Dressed Crab on Toast*

•

*Rabbit Rillettes & Cornichons
Beetroot & Watercress Salad*

•

*Slow Roast Leg of Lamb
Roast Roots
Fried Savoy Cabbage
Courgette, Mint & Butterbean Stew*

•

*Lemon Possets
Chocolate Pots
Shortbread*

INDEX

Page references for photographs are in bold

A

ale 260
almonds: pear and almond tart 218, **219**
anchovies
    anchovy toast 280
    anchovy vinaigrette 73
    boiled egg, little gem
        and anchovy 284, **285**
    sprouting broccoli and
        anchovy vinaigrette **62**, 63
Angus's birthday pickles 209
apple and plum crumble **226**, 227
Arnold Circus biscuits 246, **247**
artichokes
    artichoke heart and Berkswell
        on toast 93
    artichoke vinaigrette **168**, 169
    braised artichokes, mint
        and rocket 64, **65**
    see also Jerusalem artichokes
asparagus 170
    and butter 170
    lemon and olive oil dressing 170
    raw asparagus, fennel, chicory
        and Pecorino salad 68
aubergine and red pepper soup 44, **45**
avocado toast 32

B

bacon
    bacon buns 32
    bacon and egg pie 294, **295**
    devils on horseback 288, **289**
    see also pancetta
baked halibut with capers
    and lemon 178, **179**
baked rhubarb **38**, 39
baked whole brill 177
barbecued leg of lamb 302–3, **304–5**
bavarois: buttermilk bavarois 238
beans
    braised lamb shanks and
        haricot beans 139–40

courgette, mint and butter
    bean stew **104**, 105
green beans and roast shallots 206
beef
    Cornish pasties 293
    pan-fried calves' liver
        and radicchio **190**, 191
    roast forerib of beef 107–8
    roast sirloin 112, **113**
beer 260
    Black Velvet **258**, 259
beetroots
    beetroot soup 43
    beetroot, watercress and red onion
        salad 60–61, **61**
Bellini 259
bicicletta 256, **257**
biscuits
    Arnold Circus biscuits 246, **247**
    shortbread 239
Black Velvet **258**, 259
blinis 34
Bloody Mary 264
boiled eggs 29
    boiled egg, little gem
        and anchovy 284, **285**
bottarga: spaghetti with bottarga 153
braised artichokes, mint
    and rocket 64, **65**
braised Brussels sprouts with chestnuts
117
braised chard and fennel 202
braised courgette flowers and mint 201
braised fennel and olives **204**, 205
braised fennel sausages
    and polenta **136**, 137–8
braised lamb shanks
    and haricot beans 139–40
braised partridge, potatoes
    and pine nuts **186**, 187
brandade 94, **95**

bread
  brown bread 18
  corn bread 21
  easy bread 16, **17**
  fattoush with chicken wings 69–70, **71**
  focaccia 20
  grape bread **22**, 23
  tomato and bread soup 51
  see also buns
brill: baked whole brill 177
broccoli: sprouting broccoli
  and anchovy vinaigrette **62**, 63
brown bread 18
brownies: chocolate brownies **244**, 245
Brussels sprouts
  braised Brussels sprouts
    with chestnuts 117
  bubble and squeak 33
bubble and squeak 33
buckwheat pancakes 34
bulgar wheat: slow-roast leg of lamb
  with cracked wheat **180**, 181
buns
  bacon buns 32
  bun feast 292
  soft buns 19
butter beans: courgette, mint
  and butter bean stew **104**, 105
butterhead lettuce: butterhead, lovage
  and cucumber salad **58**, 59
buttermilk
  buttermilk bavarois 238
  lime and buttermilk tart **216**, 217
butternut squash: roasted 111

C
cabbage
  bubble and squeak 33
  cabbage and truffle spaghetti 151
  fried Savoy cabbage, garlic, parsley
    and chilli 199
  red cabbage pickle 198
cakes
  rich dark ginger cake 223
  steamed chocolate cake 224, **225**
  Turkish coffee cake 236, **237**
caldo verde 102, **103**

capers: baked halibut with capers
  and lemon 178, **179**
carrots: roasted 109
cavolo nero
  porcini and cavolo nero risotto 162, **163**
  tomato toast and cavolo nero pesto 275
celeriac
  celeriac mash 200
  celeriac rémoulade 68
  celeriac soup 46
  roasted 109
ceps *see* porcini mushrooms
ceviche: sea bass ceviche 281
champagne 259
  Bellini 259
  Black Velvet **258**, 259
  champagne cocktail 259
chard
  braised chard and fennel 202
  rainbow chard, brown rice and
    tofu tortilla 75
cheese 250–51
  artichoke heart and Berkswell
    on toast 93
  cheese straws 271
  feta and parsley parcels **282**, 283
  pizzoccheri 159
  raw asparagus, fennel, chicory
    and Pecorino salad 68
chestnuts: braised Brussels sprouts
  with chestnuts 117
chicken
  fattoush with chicken wings 69–70, **71**
  roast chicken **126**, 127–8
chicory: raw asparagus, fennel,
  chicory and Pecorino salad 68
chilli
  crab, chilli and coriander **286**, 287
  fried Savoy cabbage, garlic, parsley
    and chilli 199
chips: roast parsnip chips 274
chocolate
  chocolate brownies **244**, 245
  chocolate pots **240**, 241
  pecan and chocolate tart 214, **215**
  steamed chocolate cake 224, **225**
chorizo and potato stew 102, **103**

cider: mulled cider 260
clam, parsley and garlic
   spaghetti **156**, 157
coconut: Manea's raw fish **78**, 79
cod
   brandade 94, **95**
   salt cod and potato bake **100**, 101
   smoked cod's roe **84–5**, 86, **87**
   smoked cod's roe with
     crème fraîche **84–5**, 88
coffee
   cowboy coffee 267
   Turkish coffee cake 236, **237**
confit duck, lentil and pickled
   vegetable salad 192, **193**, 194
coriander: crab, chilli
   and coriander **286**, 287
coriander seeds: rolled pork belly, fennel
   and coriander 188, **189**
corn
   corn bread 21
   sweetcorn fritters 76, **77**
   see also polenta
Cornish pasties 293
courgettes
   braised courgette flowers
     and mint 201
   courgette frittata 80, **81**
   courgette, mint and butter
     bean stew **104**, 105
cowboy coffee 267
crab, chilli and coriander **286**, 287
crème brûlée 235
crème fraîche
   lemon and crème fraîche dressing 72
   smoked cod's roe with
     crème fraîche **84–5**, 88
crisps 269
crumble: apple and
   plum crumble **226**, 227
cucumbers
   butterhead, lovage and
     cucumber salad **58**, 59
   cured salmon with cucumber,
     mustard and dill salad 57
cured salmon with cucumber, mustard
   and dill salad 57
custard 230

D
Dark and Stormy 265
devils on horseback 288, **289**
dill: cured salmon with cucumber,
   mustard and dill salad 57
double lemon pudding **232**, 233
dressings
   anchovy vinaigrette 73
   lemon and crème fraîche dressing 72
   lemon dressing 72
   lemon and olive oil dressing 170
   vinaigrette 73
dried fruit: poached dried fruit 36
duck
   confit duck, lentil and pickled
     vegetable salad 192, **193**, 194
   duck livers and spinach on toast 83

E
eggs 28
   bacon and egg pie 294, **295**
   boiled egg, little gem
     and anchovy 284, **285**
   boiled eggs 29
   courgette frittata 80, **81**
   crème brûlée 235
   custard 230
   gull's and quail's eggs 270
   linguine carbonara 158
   poached eggs 28
   rainbow chard, brown rice
     and tofu tortilla 75
   Scotch eggs 296–7, **297**
   scrambled eggs 28
   spicy fried eggs 29

F
fattoush with chicken wings 69–70, **71**
feijoa ice cream 231
fennel
   braised chard and fennel 202
   braised fennel and olives **204**, 205
   braised fennel sausages
     and polenta **136**, 137–8
   raw asparagus, fennel, chicory
     and Pecorino salad 68
   roasted 109
   veal shin and fennel 175

fennel seeds: rolled pork belly, fennel
    and coriander 188, **189**
feta and parsley parcels **282**, 283
fish
    fish pie 97
    fish soup and rouille 54–5
    Manea's raw fish **78**, 79
    see also individual fish
flapjacks 245
focaccia 20
fried eggs 29
fried Savoy cabbage, garlic, parsley
    and chilli 199
frittata: courgette frittata 80, **81**
fritters: sweetcorn fritters 76, **77**

G
garlic
    clam, parsley and garlic
        spaghetti **156**, 157
    fried Savoy cabbage, garlic, parsley
        and chilli 199
    roasted 111
gin 261
    gimlet 261
    gin and tonic 261
    martini 262
    Negroni 261
ginger: rich dark ginger cake 223
globe artichokes *see* artichokes
granola 35
grape bread **22**, 23
green beans and roast shallots 206
Guinness 260
    Black Velvet **258**, 259
gull's eggs 270

H
haddock: fish pie 97–8
halibut: baked halibut with capers
    and lemon 178, **179**
ham: Serrano ham 272, **273**
haricot beans: braised lamb shanks
    and haricot beans 139–40
harira: lamb harira 141–3
hollandaise sauce 171

I
ice cream: feijoa ice cream 231

J
Jerusalem artichokes
    roast Jerusalem artichokes, olives
        and watercress 208
    roasted 111

K
kale: porcini and cavolo
    nero risotto 162, **163**
kipper pâté 92
Kir 256

L
lamb
    barbecued leg of lamb 302–3, **304–5**
    braised lamb shanks
        and haricot beans 139–40
    lamb harira 141–3
    roast rack of lamb 182, **183**
    slow-roast leg of lamb with
        cracked wheat **180**, 181
langoustines and mayonnaise 172–3
leek and potato soup 50
lemons
    baked halibut with capers
        and lemon 178, **179**
    double lemon pudding **232**, 233
    lemon and crème fraîche dressing 72
    lemon dressing 72
    lemon and olive oil dressing 170
    lemon possets 242, **243**
    lemon potatoes 129
    lemon spinach soup 52, **53**
    lemon tart 222
    whitebait, lemon and sage 167
lentils
    confit duck, lentil and pickled
        vegetable salad 192, **193**, 194
    lentils, roast pumpkin and
        watercress 122–3
lettuce
    boiled egg, little gem
        and anchovy 284, **285**
    butterhead, lovage and cucumber
        salad **58**, 59

lime and buttermilk tart **216**, 217
linguine carbonara 158
little gem lettuces: boiled egg, little gem
 and anchovy 284, **285**
livers
 duck livers and spinach on toast 83
 pan-fried calves' liver and
  radicchio **190**, 191
long sandwich 298–9, **300–301**
lovage: butterhead, lovage and
 cucumber salad **58**, 59

M
mackerel: smoked mackerel, potato
 and watercress salad **66**, 67
Manea's raw fish **78**, 79
margarita 265
marmalade 26
martini 262, **263**
mayonnaise: langoustines and
 mayonnaise 172–3
minestrone 47
mint
 braised artichokes, mint
  and rocket 64, **65**
 braised courgette flowers
  and mint 201
 courgette, mint and butter bean
  stew **104**, 105
 mint tea 267
Moscow Mule 264
mulled cider 260
mushrooms
 porcini and cavolo nero
  risotto 162, **163**
 potato, cep and onion bake 197
 tomato and porcini pasta 154
mustard: cured salmon with cucumber,
 mustard and dill salad 57

N
Negroni 261

O
oats
 Arnold Circus biscuits 246, **247**
 flapjacks 245
 granola 35

olives 269
 braised fennel and olives **204**, 205
 roast Jerusalem artichokes, olives
  and watercress 208
 tapenade on toast 278, **279**
onions
 beetroot, watercress and red onion
  salad 60–61, **61**
 potato, cep and onion bake 197
oranges: marmalade 26

P
Padrón peppers 271
pan-fried calves' liver
 and radicchio **190**, 191
pancakes: buckwheat pancakes 34
pancetta
 bubble and squeak 33
 linguine carbonara 158
parsley
 clam, parsley and garlic
  spaghetti **156**, 157
 feta and parsley parcels **282**, 283
 fried Savoy cabbage, garlic, parsley
  and chilli 199
 sausages and parsley
  liquor 133–4, **135**
parsnips
 roast parsnip chips 274
 roasted 111
partridges: braised partridge, potatoes
 and pine nuts **186**, 187
pasta
 cabbage and truffle spaghetti 151
 clam, parsley and garlic
  spaghetti **156**, 157
 linguine carbonara 158
 pizzoccheri 159
 spaghetti with bottarga 153
 tomato and porcini pasta 154
pasties: Cornish pasties 293
pastry
 sweet shortcrust pastry 212–13
 see also pies; tarts
pâté: kipper pâté 92
pears
 pear and almond tart 218, **219**
 poached pears 228, **229**

pecan and chocolate tart 214, **215**
Pecorino: raw asparagus, fennel, chicory
    and Pecorino salad 68
peppers
    aubergine and red pepper
        soup 44, **45**
    Padrón peppers 271
    red pepper toasts **276**, 277
pesto: tomato toast and
    cavolo nero pesto 275
pheasant: roast pheasant **114**, 115–16
pickles
    Angus's birthday pickles 209
    confit duck, lentil and pickled
        vegetable salad 192, **193**, 194
    red cabbage pickle 198
pies: bacon and egg pie 294, **295**
pine nuts: braised partridge, potatoes
    and pine nuts **186**, 187
pizzoccheri 159
plums: apple and plum
    crumble **226**, 227
poached dried fruit 36
poached eggs 28
poached pears 228, **229**
poached (or baked) rhubarb **38**, 39
poached tamarillos 234
polenta 160
    braised fennel sausages
        and polenta **136**, 137–8
    soft polenta 160
    to grill or fry 161
porcini mushrooms
    porcini and cavolo nero risotto 162, **163**
    potato, cep and onion bake 197
    tomato and porcini pasta 154
pork
    rabbit rillettes **90**, 91
    rolled pork belly, fennel
        and coriander 188, **189**
    Scotch eggs 296–7, **297**
    see also ham; sausages
possets: lemon possets 242, **243**
potatoes
    braised partridge, potatoes
        and pine nuts **186**, 187
    bubble and squeak 33
    celeriac mash 200

chorizo and potato stew 102, **103**
leek and potato soup 50
lemon potatoes 129
pizzoccheri 159
potato, cep and onion bake 197
salt cod and potato bake **100**, 101
smoked mackerel, potato
    and watercress salad **66**, 67
squid and potato stew **144**, 145–6
prunes: devils on horseback 288, **289**
pumpkin
    lentils, roast pumpkin
        and watercress 122–3
    pumpkin soup **48**, 49
    roasted 111

Q
quails: roast quails 120, **121**
quail's eggs 270

R
rabbit
    rabbit rillettes **90**, 91
    rabbit terrine **84–5**, 89
radicchio: pan-fried calves' liver
    and radicchio **190**, 191
radishes 270
rainbow chard, brown rice and tofu
    tortilla 75
raspberry shortcake tart 220–21
red cabbage pickle 198
red onions: beetroot, watercress and
    red onion salad 60–61, **61**
red peppers
    aubergine and red pepper soup
        44, **45**
    red pepper toasts **276**, 277
rhubarb: poached (or baked)
    rhubarb **38**, 39
rice
    rainbow chard, brown rice
        and tofu tortilla 75
    see also risotto
rich dark ginger cake 223
rillettes: rabbit rillettes **90**, 91
risotto: porcini and cavolo nero
    risotto 162, **163**
roast chicken **126**, 127–8

roast forerib of beef 107–8
roast Jerusalem artichokes, olives
    and watercress 208
roast parsnip chips 274
roast pheasant **114**, 115–16
roast quails 120, **121**
roast rack of lamb 182, **183**
roast roots 109–111, **110**
roast sirloin 112, **113**
roast turkey 124
    stuffing 125
rocket: braised artichokes, mint
    and rocket 64, **65**
rolled pork belly, fennel
    and coriander 188, **189**
rouille: fish soup and rouille 54–5
rum: Dark and Stormy 265

S
sage: whitebait, lemon and sage 167
salads
    beetroot, watercress
        and red onion salad 60–61, **61**
    braised artichokes, mint
        and rocket 64, **65**
    butterhead, lovage and
        cucumber salad **58**, 59
    celeriac rémoulade 68
    confit duck, lentil and pickled
        vegetable salad 192, **193**, 194
    cured salmon with cucumber,
        mustard and dill salad 57
    fattoush with chicken wings
        69–70, **71**
    raw asparagus, fennel, chicory
        and Pecorino salad 68
    smoked mackerel, potato
        and watercress salad **66**, 67
    sprouting broccoli and anchovy
        vinaigrette **62**, 63
    see also dressings
salami 269
salmon: cured salmon with cucumber,
    mustard and dill salad 57
salt cod
    brandade 94, **95**
    salt cod and potato bake **100**, 101

sandwiches: long sandwich
    298–9, **300–301**
sausagemeat: stuffing 125
sausages 269
    braised fennel sausages
        and polenta **136**, 137–8
    bubble and squeak 33
    chorizo and potato stew 102, **103**
    sausages and parsley liquor
        133–4, **135**
Savoy cabbage, garlic, parsley
    and chilli 199
Scotch eggs 296–7, **297**
scrambled eggs 28
sea bass ceviche 281
Serrano ham 272, **273**
shallots: green beans
    and roast shallots 206
shortbread 239
shortcake: raspberry shortcake tart
    220–21
shortcrust pastry 212–13
slow-roast leg of lamb with
    cracked wheat **180**, 181
smoked cod's roe **84–5**, 86, **87**
    with crème fraîche **84–5**, 88
smoked mackerel, potato
    and watercress salad **66**, 67
soups
    aubergine and red pepper soup
        44, **45**
    beetroot soup 43
    celeriac soup 46
    fish soup and rouille 54–5
    leek and potato soup 50
    lemon spinach soup 52, **53**
    minestrone 47
    pumpkin soup **48**, 49
    tomato and bread soup 51
spaghetti
    cabbage and truffle spaghetti 151
    clam, parsley and garlic spaghetti
        156, 157
    spaghetti with bottarga 153
spicy fried eggs 29
spinach
    duck livers and spinach on toast 83
    lemon spinach soup 52, **53**

sprouting broccoli and anchovy
    vinaigrette **62**, 63
sprouts *see* Brussels sprouts
squid and potato stew **144**, 145–6
steamed chocolate cake 224, **225**
stuffing 125
sumac: fattoush with
    chicken wings 69–70, **71**
sweet shortcrust pastry 212–13
sweetcorn fritters 76, **77**
Swiss chard: braised chard
    and fennel 202

T
tamarillos: poached tamarillos 234
tapenade on toast 278, **279**
tarts
    lemon tart 222
    lime and buttermilk tart **216**, 217
    pear and almond tart 218, **219**
    pecan and chocolate tart 214, **215**
    raspberry shortcake tart 220–21
tea: mint tea 267
tequila: margarita 265
terrine: rabbit terrine **84–5**, 89
tofu: rainbow chard, brown rice
    and tofu tortilla 75
tomatoes
    tomato and bread soup 51
    tomato and porcini pasta 154
    tomato toast and
        cavolo nero pesto 275
tortillas: rainbow chard, brown rice
    and tofu tortilla 75

truffle oil: cabbage
    and truffle spaghetti 151
turkey
    roast turkey 124
    stuffing 125
Turkish coffee cake 236, **237**

V
veal shin and fennel 175
venison stew 147–9, **149**
vinaigrette 73
    anchovy vinaigrette 73
    artichoke vinaigrette **168**, 169
vodka 264
    Bloody Mary 264
    martini 262
    Moscow Mule 264

W
watercress
    beetroot, watercress and
        red onion salad 60–61, **61**
    lentils, roast pumpkin
        and watercress 122–3
    roast Jerusalem artichokes,
        olives and watercress 208
    smoked mackerel, potato
        and watercress salad **66**, 67
whisky 266
whitebait, lemon and sage 167
wine cocktails 256

Y
yoghurt 37

Acknowledgements

I would like to give very special thanks to Brian and Elizabeth Henderson, my dear in-laws, fantastic hosts in every way possible. Annabelle and Stephen Harty – in the words of Kevin Costner, 'Build a field and they will come.' My mum, Pauline Harper, a wonderful, wise woman. Melanie Arnold – well, where would I begin, the calm and gentle force behind Rochelle Canteen and A & H.

And all the following brilliant people who over many years have taught me to cook, mainly by my scouring through their books, or who have encouraged me to write this book, so a big thank you. Also my darling kids, Hector, Owen and Frances, for their fantastic appetites. I know there are many others, so big thanks to you as well.

Stephanie Alexander, Juliet Annan, Catherine Barraclough, Mike Belben, Ben's Fish, April Bloomfield, Maddalena Bonnino, Nathan Burton, Harvey Cabaniss, Camisa, Martin Cohen, Sadie Coles, Angus Cook, Ben Coombs, Ania Cwikla, Pauline Daly, Ronnie di Stasio, David Eyre, James Ferguson, Charles Fontaine, Alcides Gauto, Justin Piers Gellatly, Peter Gordon, Rose Gray, Trevor Gulliver, Mark Hix, Simon Hopkinson, Jonathan Jones, Leila Khattar, Pierre Koffman, Annie Lee, Jeremy Lee, Giorgio Locatelli, Sarah Lucas, Ayliffe Maddever, Leila McAlister, McKanna Meats, Mary-Sue Milliken, Sophie Missing, James Moores, Thomas Oppong, Alethea Palmer, Bren Parkins-Knight, Jonathan Rutherford-Best, Alyona Sevidova, Justine Short, Ellie Smith, Jon Spiteri, Douglas Stewart, St John and all who sail in her, Alice Waters, Joe Woodhouse, Paula Woolfit.

And everyone else at Rochelle Canteen and Arnold & Henderson, past and present.